Stefan Buczacki

Best
Clematis

Special Photography Andrew Lawson

HAMLYN

Publishing Director Laura Bamford
Creative Director Keith Martin
Design Manager Bryan Dunn
Designer TT Designs
Executive Editor Julian Brown
Editor Karen O'Grady
Production Julie Hadingham
Picture Research Liz Fowler
Researcher Liz Dobbs
Special Photography Andrew Lawson

First published in Great Britain in 1998
by Hamlyn
an imprint of Octopus Publishing Group Limited
Michelin House, 81 Fulham Road,
London SW3 6RB

© Octopus Publishing Group Limited 1998
Text © Stefan Buczacki 1998
Design © Octopus Publishing Group Limited 1998

Produced by Toppan
Printed in China

A catalogue record for this book is available from
the British Library

ISBN 0 600 59370 3

CONTENTS

INTRODUCTION

Clematis is one of those ancient words that have been adapted and adopted by modern science. As with many of these words, there are various opinions over exactly what it meant or how it was derived. *Klematis* was unarguably a Greek word and was used by the Greek author Dioscorides. He used it to mean an unspecified climbing plant, possibly distinguished simply by being woody if, as is often said, the name was derived from *klema*, a twig. But if you accept the alternative theory that *klema* meant a tendril, then it seems that the Greeks were referring to *Clematis* as we know it today.

Clematis, or at least most of them, are tendril climbers, the tendrils being modified leaves used for grasping a support. The group belongs, rather unexpectedly, in the buttercup family Ranunculaceae. Also their flowers have no petals: the glorious colours that we see and admire appear are the sepals which, in most 'conventional' flowers, are green and lie outside the petals but are here modified to resemble real petals. They are known, more correctly, as petaloid sepals.

It's no surprise that Dioscorides and his compatriots should have known *Clematis* because several types occur naturally in the Mediterranean area. There are probably 10 European species; not many perhaps out of a total of over 200 in the genus, but most have contributed importantly to the development of garden varieties. And their existence has meant that clematis have been an important part of European gardening for many centuries. Outside Europe, *Clematis* species occur widely throughout the northern temperate regions, to a lesser extent in the south-ern temperate regions and even extend into high mountain areas in Tropical Africa. Most significantly, many species occur in China, the Himalayas and adjoining regions. This meant that there was a rich harvest of new plants for the collectors of the 19th century, Robert Fortune, William Purdom, Ernest Wilson and others, to bring back to the West. But it also meant that *Clematis* was able to enter Oriental gardening at an early date and, in Japan especially, varieties had been selected for centuries before Europeans first saw them. Many of the very important large-flowered, summer-blooming hybrids are derived from Japanese varieties that were well advanced garden plants by the 19th century.

The garden clematis of today are relatively easy plants to grow and certainly much more versatile than is sometimes imagined. Their site requirements are fairly undemanding. Most grow best in a fairly rich, moist, loamy soil, ideally neutral or slightly alkaline. They are less successful in acidic soils and are highly tolerant, although not demanding, of fairly high alkalinity.

Most clematis are climbers, although of greatly varying vigour. I would, indeed, suggest that the main reason why gardeners sometimes feel dissatisfied with clematis is that they have planted them in inappropriate situations. The very vigorous varieties, which tend to be smaller flowered, really should be allowed the freedom of a semi-natural part of the garden; they are inappropriate, difficult and cumbersome when confined to the neatness of house-wall trellis. In such places, a less vigorous, preferably larger-flowered variety is more in keeping. I've laid considerable emphasis in the individual plant entries on the ways in which clematis could best be incorporated into the overall garden display.

Clematis are already the most popular climbing plants for gardens. I certainly don't need to promote them in that respect. What I hope is that this book will encourage gardeners to use a much wider variety of clematis than they have hitherto considered; or had even believed to exist. And I hope also that by increasing demand from potential purchasers, I can encourage nurseries and garden centres to offer more of the currently less-familiar forms, especially among the species.

I have divided the book more or less according to the species from which particular groups of varieties have been derived. This generally reflects flowering time and pruning treatment required. I have grown a large number of different clematis over the years and have seen most of those that I haven't. Many of the varieties that I recommend will be widely available; some may need searching for. In some groups, there are many rather similar types and it may help you in making your choice if you look first at those that have been granted the Award of Garden Merit (AGM) by the Royal Horticultural Society. This at least indicates that the plant has been grown under carefully observed garden conditions and has proved itself worthy. But be aware also, as I mention in some instances, that the form of the plant given the award may not be available at all nurseries; there are meritorious and non-meritorious versions of some variable species.

Clematis **'Comtesse de Bouchaud'**

4

SOIL AND SITE

Soil

Growing conditions for climbers of all types are rather more exacting than for most other groups of garden plant, because the soil close to their support is likely to be impoverished in some way. If they are planted against a wall or fence, the soil will be dry as it is sheltered to a considerable degree from rain. And if the support is provided by a hedge or a tree, the situation will be compounded by a shortage of nutrients. Once the climber is established, regular feeding and watering will help maintain it in a healthy state (see page 13), but initial preparation before planting is vitally important if your plant really is to produce of its best.

It's worth looking at the way in which different soils vary to see how far they fall short of the ideal for clematis; and how they can be improved. All soils contain greater or lesser amounts of sand, silt, clay and humus and the relative proportions of these components give each soil type its characteristic features. A soil with a high clay content is slow to warm up in spring but it then retains warmth well; it's also likely to be generously supplied with nutrients. In dry conditions, however, such as those in which clematis tend to grow, it can be hard and impenetrable whereas in wet winter weather, it may become waterlogged. By contrast, a light sandy soil will warm up quickly, cool down quickly and, being free draining, lose both water and nutrients rapidly. Humus (part-decomposed organic matter) will improve both types of soil, for it contains natural glues that bind together soil particles to form crumbs, and it also helps with the retention of

moisture because of its sponge-like properties. Always dig in plenty of compost or other organic matter before planting (see page 15).

But there's another aspect of soils that is especially important with all types of clematis: their relative acidity or alkalinity. This is usually expressed as the pH, measured on a scale from 0 to 14. Soils with a pH above 7 are alkaline, those with a pH below 7, acid. Most soils are naturally somewhere between about pH 6 and pH 7.5 (more or less neutral) and most plants will thrive in these conditions. But there are exceptions.

Clematis are among the most important garden plants that tolerate more alkaline conditions and, although soils around neutral will be perfectly adequate, any soil with a pH below about 6 will be too acid and should be altered by adding garden lime before planting. The amount of lime to add depends, not only on the initial pH, but also on the texture and structure of the soil. This information should be given on the bag. Garden lime or ground limestone (finely ground calcium carbonate) is the most convenient form of lime to use and is best applied in the autumn. A few years after application, the acidity may rise again, largely as a result of the use of acidic fertilizer. It's worth checking the soil close to the plant from time to time, therefore, with a pH testing kit;

Clematis **'Marie Boisselot'**

especially if the overall performance of the plant begins to decline in a garden known to be naturally acidic.

The kits available to gardeners for testing soil pH are of variable reliability and my recommendation is to use one based on the colour change of a chemical dye, often using indicator papers. Small pH meters sold for garden use are less effective and they don't measure pH directly.

Site

Aspect is important for growing clematis but only in so far as you must choose the most appropriate type for each situation. One of the great virtues of clematis is their diversity and the fact that, soil and other conditions being appropriate, there is a variety for almost every garden position. I have indicated under the individual descriptions the most appropriate position for each type.

Along with their varying tolerance of different aspects, there are varying degrees of shade tolerance but two general points are worth making here. All clematis will grow better if the lower part of the stem and the roots are relatively cool. Even those growing in full sun will benefit from the provision of some shade over the soil; often this can be achieved simply by placing old tiles and a thick layer of mulch over the soil surface. And some of the large-flowered varieties, in particular, will produce better and more intense flower colour if the upper part of the plant is in very lightly dappled shade rather than the full glare of the sun. Remember that many are derived from plants that naturally grow in woodland.

Clematis **'Ville de Lyon'**

All clematis require some form of support; that is in the very nature of climbing plants. Even the herbaceous species have insufficiently strong stems to be free standing but I consider them separately in the relevant part of the book on page 82. For the remainder, the genuine climbing types, you have a range of options.

Other plants

This is the most informal way of growing clematis; it is the way that most species grow naturally and can look extremely attractive. It is important, however, to choose plants of complementary vigour: a clematis that grows 3m (10ft) high in a season is an inappropriate choice to scramble over a shrub only 1m (3ft) tall, and a very vigorous clematis can cause harm to a relatively young tree. Both evergreen and deciduous support plants may be used; a small-flowered clematis, for instance, looks particularly attractive when growing over or through a dark-leaved conifer or similar evergreen. Some small-flowered clematis, like the early-flowering *macropetala* types, can also look very pretty when threading their way through heathers, whereas others, like the late-flowering *viticella* varieties, look better cascading down from the branches of a low tree. On trees with fairly long, clear lengths of trunk, some tying in will almost certainly be necessary to assist the clematis to reach the lowest limbs, but thereafter no further artificial help should be needed. It is when dead trees or stumps are used as support for clematis, however, that the greatest problems can arise. An entire dead tree will very soon become unstable, an instability hastened by the growth of the clematis on it. Unless it is a very durable hardwood, such as an oak, the wood will decay after a few years and a gale can bring the entire structure, clematis and all, crashing to the ground. Cutting the tree down to leave a length of stump over which to grow a clematis may minimise the likely physical damage

Clematis viticella

if it falls, but the loss of an important garden feature is still frustrating. And in the case of non-coniferous trees, a dead stump can easily act as a focus for infection of the site by honey fungus, with disastrous consequences for the garden as a whole.

The classic combination is clematis with climbing roses. I think they create a wonderful image but would counsel two words of caution. Do look very carefully at the colour combinations before you plant; and do choose the later flowering clematis that require relatively hard pruning and can be cut back at the same time as the climbing rose.

Walls

Walls are obvious supports for climbers; and almost any type of wall will suffice although it is as well to be sure that the mortar and the bricks or stonework are sound, especially if the wall is tall. House walls are what I call too formal, however, for rampant, 'wild' clematis, like *Clematis montana*. A boundary wall or old outbuilding is much more appropriate for them. The plants will need something to which they can be tied; either trellis or wire. Use plastic coated wire specially intended for the purpose: wire that can be tensioned without snapping. For most clematis, wire 2mm (⅛in) thick will suffice; it is best attached to looped vine eyes, screwed into wall plugs.

Trellis

Trellis has the merit of providing a fairly attractive wall covering even when the clematis itself may be leafless and bare.

But it is important to attach it to 2cm (¾in) thick battens in order to raise it from the wall surface, and important also to select a type that is strong enough for the purpose. The rather appealing diamond-patterned wooden trellis is fine for most clematis except the very vigorous types, like *C. montana* or some of the Oriental late-flowering species. Personally, I avoid like the plague the plastic so-called 'clematis netting', one of the least attractive intrusions into modern gardening.

Trellis can also be used very effectively as infilling panels for open framework arches, arbours, summerhouses, small pavilions and low fences. And in all of these situations, clematis may be planted to scramble over it. But do use strong, robust trellis made from durable timber that really will still be standing when your clematis are mature. Remember, too, that while a painted wooden structure can be most attractive, it will be only be really practical if it is clothed with a clematis that requires hard annual pruning; that is, one of the late flowering types. Otherwise, the whole becomes impossible ever to repaint and begins to look simply shabby.

Archways

I have always thought that archways play a very valuable role in gardens. Positioned over path corners or used as focal points, they can add interest to the garden and help to divide it into discrete areas, each with its own character. But an archway is naked without a climber and they are ideal for clematis. Purpose-built archways are obtainable made from metal, usually painted

Clematis **'Miss Bateman'**

or plastic coated, and these are generally best in a more formal garden. Wooden structures are most appropriate for rural settings but whether the wood used is planed timber, or (and better I think) round rustic poles, it should have been pressure treated with preservative. Vertical posts should be sunk 45-60cm (18-24in) in the ground and rammed in hard without concreting. All verticals should be braced with diagonals.

Pergolas

A pergola is simply an open framework for the support of climbers. It is especially effective for supporting that most attractive combination of clematis and

Clematis montana var. rubens

climbing roses. The very finest have brick pillars and wooden crosspieces but perfectly acceptable versions for smaller gardens are built entirely from wood, applying similar criteria as for an archway. The main danger when constructing a pergola is that insufficient attention is paid to its lateral support and the whole is built in a single very long run, and thus has inherent instability. Arranging for the pergola to include at least one right-angled turn will help it structurally.

Pillars

The pillar is the simplest of all climbing plant supports, consisting of a single upright structure around which the clematis is tied and trained. The commonest, and in many ways most practical and attractive, are lengths of hardwood tree trunk, about 2m (6-7ft) tall and sunk firmly into the ground. It is essential, however, to use a durable hardwood, such as oak, or a pressure-treated softwood; otherwise the base will rot and render the whole thing unstable just at the moment when your clematis reaches maturity.

Tripods and obelisks

The tripod and the obelisk are, I think, the most under-used and under-appreciated of clematis supports, although they are seen commonly enough in large public gardens and can easily be copied. The ideal height for a tripod or obelisk is about 2m (6-7ft); tripods are best made of rustic poles, obelisks of sectioned and painted wood, reminiscent of the lovely structures so popular in Tudor and Medieval times.

Clematis 'Princess Diana'

Clematis in containers

Perhaps the biggest change in clematis growing in recent years has resulted from the realisation that they can be very successful in containers. I had been as guilty as anyone in believing that they really weren't happy when grown in this way; they were too deeply rooted, the compost can't be kept sufficiently and uniformly moist the list of objections went on. All that has now altered and I, like many other gardeners, grow them satisfactorily in large tubs. It's important to use a good quality soil-based compost; John Innes No 3 is ideal. My experience has been that a soil-less compost is useless. The containers should be not less than 20cm (8in) in diameter and depth; 30cm (12in) is much better. The container should be shaded in order to keep the roots cool and the compost should be well mulched early in the season. Feed the plants exactly as you would clematis growing in the open garden (see opposite).

Support for clematis growing in containers is achieved either by using one of the purpose-made sections of trellis, usually kite-shaped, now available; which I think look frankly dreadful, or by an arrangement of tripod or obelisk style supports; which looks and functions immeasurably better.

I hope that more gardeners will experiment with growing clematis in containers; almost any except the most vigorous types are worth trying, although the large-flowered summer-blooming hybrids generally work best.

Clematis armandii **'Apple Blossom'**

An old gardening friend who has grown clematis for over 60 years used to tell me that I should remember one fact and one alone if I wanted a really outstanding display: 'Clematis', he would say, 'are greedy feeders.' I believe he was right, and yet I doubt if there is any other important group of garden plants where feeding is so neglected.

And indeed, seeing wild clematis growing in woodland or scrambling over rocks, you may be forgiven for wondering why any feeding is necessary as, in their natural habitat, they seem to be thriving in pretty impoverished conditions. The answer is quite simply that there are also few genera where the difference between the wild plant (or neglected garden plant) on the one hand and the well fed individual on the other, is so marked. So while clematis will grow and flower with no additional fertilizer; my belief is that their overall life and effectiveness will be very much more limited if they are neglected.

Indeed, I find that with climbers in general, but clematis especially, the improvement after feeding is sometimes so great that gardeners scarcely recognise their own plants. But what is the correct feed to use and how frequently should it be applied? Let's first look briefly at what constitutes a fertilizer.

Fertilizers

Almost every fertilizer contains three main ingredients: nitrogen (N), phosphorus or phosphate (P) and potash (K). Nitrogen encourages leafy growth and is the key element, because healthy foliage is essential for an overall healthy plant. Phosphate is especially valuable in encouraging root development and so is very useful at planting time to aid initial establishment. Potash plays an important part in promoting flowering and fruiting, especially significant with a flowering ornamental like clematis. Most blended fertilizers also contain greater or lesser amounts of other, minor nutrients like magnesium, calcium and boron.

One other nutrient, however, is particularly important. Iron helps in the process by which the green colouring matter, chlorophyll, is manufactured but plants find it difficult to take up iron from alkaline soils as it becomes chemically attached to other elements. It's true that, as they are naturally adapted to alkaline soils, clematis can absorb iron better than plants than naturally prefer acidic conditions but I still like to give them an extra boost of iron fertilizer every spring. It's important, however, to use a fertilizer containing sequestered iron; that is, iron in an organic form that does not become chemically 'locked up' in the soil

Feeding

Using the information that I have given about fertilizer content, it's not difficult to work out a feeding regime for your clematis. When you plant them, use a fertilizer with a high phosphate content; bone meal, applied as a good handful to the planting hole is ideal. Thereafter, in early spring, I give my plants a dose of sequestered iron and then, a little later, a handful of a proprietary rose fertilizer. These are blended mixtures, available with either artificial or organic ingredients. They have a high potash content, almost invariably with added magnesium and trace elements too. But there's not much point in simply depositing dry fertilizer powder around a plant growing in inherently dry soil, for it will remain on the surface, become caked and provide no benefit for the plant. Ideally, therefore, it should be applied after rain, raked into the soil surface and then be watered-in with a watering can or hose.

During the summer when the plants are growing rapidly, I give two or three applications of a proprietary soluble fertilizer. Applied as liquid, these are absorbed very rapidly, and almost all general-purpose blends, as well as special tomato feeds, contain a desirably high proportion of potash.

In order to try and maintain the soil around established clematis in a moist condition, a mulch should be put on in spring and again in autumn. But do remember that the soil must be wet initially; a mulch will keep a dry soil dry just as much as it will a wet one. By and large, the most useful mulching material for clematis is home-produced garden compost or leaf mould; in my experience, well rotted manure is not as effective and you should certainly avoid very acidic organic materials such as peat or conifer needles.

During dry weather in summer, additional water should be supplied; if hose-pipes are not permitted, then a watering can full every week should be sufficient; provided that there is still mulch in place to cut down on evaporation loss.

I'm sure it's true that most gardeners propagate plants such as clematis out of enjoyment rather than necessity. It's rather infrequently that we are likely to want large quantities of a particular variety or that we can't afford to buy a well grown plant from a nursery. Nonetheless, an extra one or two may come in handy; or perhaps you can exchange a variety with your neighbour. And plant propagation for its own sake is always satisfying.

There is, however, a considerable difference in the ease with which various clematis types can be propagated. As with all other groups of plant, true species may be propagated from seed; with clematis, this is relatively straightforward (see Box on page 16). The result will be flowering plants, perfectly recognisable as clematis although some 'come true' more reliably than others meaning that the progeny may be more or less different from their parents.

As with hybrids and selected varieties of other plants, 'true-to-type' propagation is achieved by vegetative means, because the tissues of the offspring are identical to those of the parent. The three commonest methods of vegetative propagation are grafting, layering and cuttings. Grafting is performed infrequently with clematis although it is useful with those large-flowered hybrids that are stubbornly resistant to other method of propagation. The native *Clematis vitalba* or *C. viticella* are usually chosen as rootstocks.

For most plants, however, cuttings offer much the preferred method. Nonetheless, while the species and many small-flowered hybrids will root with considerable ease, the large-flowered summer-blooming hybrids can be very difficult to strike, at least other than with commercial facilities. Layering is relatively successful, if slow, with most types.

LEFT: *Clematis* 'Etoile Violette'

ABOVE: *Clematis* 'Ernest Markham'

Cuttings

With all types of clematis, cuttings of semi-ripe wood should be removed from the parent plant in late spring or early summer, using a neat cut midway between nodes. Clematis are the most important exceptions to the general rule that cuttings should be taken immediately below a node. This is because they have the greatest concentration of natural root-promoting hormones between, rather than at their nodes. Although the cut should, however, be made midway between the nodes, the cutting should be pushed into the growing medium up to the level of the node.

Clematis cuttings should be rooted (or 'struck') in a covered chamber, either a propagator as used for seed sowing or a covered cold-frame. It's very important to maintain a moist atmosphere around the cuttings for they will otherwise lose water through their leaves at a time when, lacking roots, they are unable to replace it from below.

Even with a covered propagator, therefore, you should pay careful attention to the moisture content of the rooting medium and use a hand sprayer to mist over the cuttings regularly. Cuttings may be rooted directly into sand or, in a cold-frame, into soil, although for clematis, I always use a 50:50 mixture (by volume) of horticultural sand and John Innes soil-based seedling compost.

Layering

The difficulty of striking some clematis from cuttings can often be overcome by layering: anchoring a stem into the soil, or into a pot of compost sunk to its rim, while it is still attached to the parent plant. A small piece of bent wire will suffice to hold it down. The disadvantage is that some patience is needed as, in my experience, clematis layerings rarely root satisfactorily in less than 12 months.

SEED

Packeted seed of some types of clematis has become available from seed companies in recent years; the small-flowered, yellow-flowered late summer species like *C. tangutica* are those most frequently seen in the lists of general seed companies, although I have seen more specialist suppliers offer 20 or more species, including evergreen and tender forms. But never forget that it's always worth using seed obtained fresh from your own or friends' plants; fresh seed is often much more successful than packeted.

Use a soil-based seedling compost, very lightly cover the seeds with compost and keep them in a propagator or cold frame, ideally at a temperature not exceeding 20°C (68°F). Germination will usually be slow and erratic over a period of several months.

ABOVE: *Clematis tangutica*

RIGHT: *Clematis alpina* 'Frances Rivis'

Why the pruning of clematis puzzles so many people is a continuing mystery to me. Yet I have been asked more questions about the pruning of clematis than about any other single type of plant; even roses. In reality, it is no more difficult and certainly no less logical than any other pruning; although I do think it would help a great deal if people thought of clematis as long, thin, flowering shrubs. So with this, perhaps novel, notion in mind, let's remind ourselves of the basic logic and reasoning behind the pruning of any woody plant. There are two questions to consider: when and by how much?

The timing of pruning is dictated first by flowering time, second by the effect that the winter may have on the plant, and third, the time of year when the plant is growing most vigorously.

With clematis, flowering time is much the most important of these, for clematis bear their flowers in one of two ways: either on wood produced during the previous growing season or on wood produced during the current year. Common sense will tell you which is which. If a clematis flowers early in the year, it will clearly be unable to do so on wood produced during that year; there will have been insufficient time for this to develop. So the flowers are borne on old wood: that produced in the previous or earlier years. The spring flowering species, including *Clematis alpina*, *C. macropetala*, *C. montana* and their varieties, are the most important of these but the early-summer-blooming, large-flowered hybrids also flower in this way.

By contrast, those clematis that bloom later, after midsummer, bear their flowers on the current season's

Clematis macropetala **'Blue Bird'**

wood. The most important of these are the late summer and autumn-flowering species such as the Oriental *C. tangutica*, the American *C. texensis*, European *C. campaniflora*, the wonderful varieties derived from *C. viticella* and also the later-summer-blooming, large-flowered hybrids.

As we don't want to remove flower buds before they have done their job, pruning is performed *after* flowering.

But should you do so immediately after flowering, or wait a little longer? The general rule is that the early-season clematis, those that flower on the old wood, should be pruned immediately after the flowers fade. By contrast, those that flower after midsummer on the wood of the current season should be pruned at some time between late autumn and the end of late winter or the start of early spring. By and large,

Clematis viticella 'Purpurea Plena Elegans'

Group 1

Group 1 clematis flower early in the year but on wood produced in the previous season. Prune immediately after flowering by cutting back all weak and dead stems to just above a node. Any tangled or excessive growth should also be cut back but large, well-established plants that are growing where they may be allowed free rein need not be pruned at all. Conversely, a plant that has truly become a tangled mass may be pruned back as hard as a Group 2 or even a Group 3 plant, and will regenerate successfully although, in the latter case, all of one year's flower buds will, of course, be removed.

the spring is preferable as the newly cut shoots are not then subjected to the rigours of the winter and the possibility of frost penetrating through the pruning cuts.

I can reduce this information to my rules of thumb for pruning clematis and if you forget everything else in this part of the book, do please remember these and you will never go far wrong. First, prune all clematis in the spring; in early spring if they are summer or autumn-flowering types, but slightly later, as the flowers are fading, if they are spring-flowering varieties. And second, the later in the year that your particular variety flowers, the harder should you prune it.

But for those wanting a little more detail, read on. Because, bearing the above logic in mind, all clematis species and varieties can be placed into one of three pruning groups and throughout the book I have indicated this under each entry.

Clematis montana 'Elizabeth'

Group 2

Group 2 clematis flower early in the summer and, like the Group 1 varieties, they also flower on the previous season's wood and like them, they should be pruned in early spring by cutting out any dead or weak stems. As they flower rather later than Group 1 varieties, however, they require rather harder pruning, so cut back the remaining shoots by about 30cm (12in), cutting to just above a pair of plump buds. Any dead leaf stalks should be trimmed away and the plant generally tidied up.

Clematis montana **'Marjorie'**

Clematis montana var. *sericea*

Clematis **'Ascotiensis'**

Group 3

Group 3 clematis flower later in the summer on the current year's wood and they should also be pruned early in the spring, but, since they flower later, they should be pruned much more severely. All of the previous season's growth should be cut back to just above a pair of plump buds positioned about 75cm (30in) above soil level. If there is so much top growth that it will be blown around in the winter, however, the bulk may be cut back in late autumn, leaving the final tidying until the spring.

Clematis **'Madame Julia Correvon'**

PESTS, DISEASES AND OTHER PROBLEMS

Clematis aren't especially prone to pests and diseases; indeed, were it not for the puzzling and frustrating disease called clematis wilt, they would be relatively trouble-free. My key should enable you, however, to identify all of the common problems and find a solution relatively easily. Clematis wilt is, nonetheless, special and it's worth looking at in some more detail.

When clematis wilt strikes, the younger leaves suddenly droop, the upper parts of the leaf stalks blacken and the affected leaves then wither and die, the entire process sometimes taking only a few days. Discoloured lesions may occur on the stem at or near ground level and dark patches also appear on some otherwise healthy-looking leaves. Before long, almost all of the above-ground parts of the plant have wilted and died back. There are rather marked differences in varietal susceptibility; the species, both early and late flowering are rarely affected with any severity. I have never seen it on herbaceous clematis and suspect they may be immune. The large-flowered summer-blooming hybrids are almost always the worst affected, those derived from *Clematis lanuginosa* seemingly the most severely of all.

Despite its familiarity and severity, very little is known about the biology of the condition. The stem lesions are caused by a fungus now called *Ascochyta clematidina* which may originate from the soil, other plants or from the leaf patches. Infection possibly occurs in conditions of high humidity through small wounds caused by insects, wind damage or even stem ties, but there's no extensive fungal development within the plant tissues. As the cause and biology are so incompletely known, it's difficult to recommend reliable control measures, but it is important to avoid mechanical damage to clematis stems, particularly from securing ties.

Proprietary fungicidal sprays sold for mildew control on ornamental plants may help to suppress the fungus on the leaves but are not worth applying as preventative treatments.

Assuming that an attack has been observed, the best plan is to cut back the plant to soil level or just below; and then wait. Quite commonly, new shoots arise and are unaffected by the disease and the plant recovers. If the symptoms do recur, however, remove the soil to a depth of about 30cm (12in) around the affected site and replace it with fresh soil before planting a new plant. It's also sensible always to plant clematis up to 15cm (6in) deeper in the soil than indicated by the soil mark on the stem. This encourages the formation of roots from the lower part of the stem and these appear to be less liable to become infected. If the disease does reappear, then switch to growing species rather than large-flowered hybrids.

Clematis **'Prince Charles'**

KEY TO COMMON PROBLEMS ON CLEMATIS

Symptom	Cause	Treatment
Leaves and/or other parts with powdery white coating	Powdery mildew	Use proprietary approved fungicide spray
Leaves variously mottled or malformed	Viruses	No treatment necessary
Leaves bleached (chlorotic); often with veins dark green	Iron deficiency (only on very alkaline soils)	Apply sequestered iron fertilizer (see page 13)
Leaves wilt; shoots and entire plant may die back	Clematis wilt	See text
Leaves sticky and sooty; leaves and stems infested by colonies of small wingless and winged insects	Aphids	Use proprietary approved pesticide spray
Leaves with small, ragged holes, especially at tips of shoot; buds sometimes killed	Earwigs	Trap insects by placing upturned plant pots stuffed with hay on top of bamboo canes close to the plants. The earwigs will hide in the pots during the daytime and can then be collected and destroyed.
Leaves sticky and sooty; stems and undersides of leaves infested by brown or yellow scales	Scale insects	Wait until plant is pruned, then prune harder than usual to remove all affected material and destroy it.
Leaves with small notches eaten out of edges	Weevils	No treatment necessary
Flowers small, malformed and green, especially apparent on the first formed flowers of pale-coloured varieties.	Abnormally cold weather at an early stage of flower development appears to be partially responsible but infection by a mycoplasma (a kind of sub-microscopic organism) may also be involved.	No treatment possible
Shoots eaten at or just above soil level, leaves with irregular holes, slime trails present. Young shoots emerging in spring are especially prone.	Slugs and snails or woodlice	Use slug pellets or other approved treatment close to the plants. In early spring, place spiny twigs around the base of the stems.

EARLY-FLOWERING SPECIES

These clematis flower in spring on stems produced during the previous year. The first to appear are the *alpina* and *macropetala* varieties followed by the *montana* types. I have also included here a selection of some more uncommon early-flowering species that should be more widely grown, and that may be obtained from clematis specialists. All produce a mass of rather small flowers, so creating a very obvious and characteristic impression of a plant covered with bloom. Each individual flower is less showy than those of the summer hybrids, but many gardeners prefer this more natural look.

The early-flowering species are natural ramblers and may be allowed to do so uninhibited and unpruned, as they would in their native habitats. If you do wish to control them in confined spaces, they may be pruned as Group 1 types (see page 19).

The *alpina* and *macropetala* varieties offer a wide choice of easy to grow clematis that combine well with other plants. Both have similar growth habits and requirements; indeed so similar are they that some varieties flit from one genus to another, depending on which catalogue or book you consult. The practical difference lies in the flower shape: the *alpina* varieties have nodding, bell-shaped flowers while the *macropetala* types have semi-double flowers with slightly more flared bells. Both have attractive seedheads from late spring onwards; and a bonus for the flower arranger is that these appear at a warm, dry time of year, so they are ideal for preserving in glycerine. The *montana* varieties and their relatives are more vigorous, and ideal for quickly disguising walls or tree stumps.

Clematis alpina 'Frances Rivis'

Clematis alpina types

❝ *I rather think that* Clematis alpina *has made me more friends than most garden plants. Over the years, gardeners up and down the land have asked me for an interesting climbing plant, none too vigorous, for a cool, shady aspect, quite commonly a position close to the front door of their house. And it's been one of the* C. alpina *varieties that I've chosen to satisfy their request. It's an interesting plant in that, although a native of Europe (it occurs naturally in much of northern Europe and Asia as well as mountainous regions further south), it wasn't introduced to British gardens until as recently as 1792. Oddly enough, however, the white or cream-flowered variant from north-east Europe, now called sub-species* sibirica *has a slightly longer history in cultivation and was in gardens before 1753. This goes to prove that, sadly, the early-flowering clematis as a group were rather late and rather slow to be fully appreciated. Still the best and most celebrated form of* C. alpina *is 'Frances Rivis' although it was as late as 1965 that it was granted its original AGM. A number of additional varieties, including several with flowers close to dark red have appeared over the past few years and more may be expected.* ❞

PRUNING: Group I

SITE AND SOIL: Tolerant of all aspects so very useful for cool, shady walls where most other clematis are not suitable. A moisture-retentive, slightly alkaline soil is preferred.

HARDINESS: Very hardy, tolerating at least -20°C (-4°F) in winter.

SIZE: 3-5m (10-16ft) after three or four years. They can be grown on 1-2m (3-6ft) high fences, however, as once they reach the top of the fence, the stems will cascade down most attractively.

PROPAGATION: Fairly easy, from semi-ripe cuttings in late summer, layering or seed.

ABOVE: *Clematis alpina* 'Helsingborg'   BELOW: *Clematis alpina* 'Ruby'

Clematis alpina 'Willy'

Clematis alpina ssp. *sibirica* 'White Moth'

Easy to Grow
Spring Flowers
Attractive Seedheads
Not Too Vigorous

■ **GARDEN USES** The *alpina* varieties are very natural-looking clematis, so are best used in informal plantings: allow them to ramble over shrubs or clothe pergola posts, fences or walls. They are not too vigorous so make ideal partners for small and medium-sized shrubs, up to about 3m (10ft). A cold wall or fence could, for example, be brightened up in spring by a wall-trained Japanese flowering quince (*Chaenomeles* x *superba* or *C. speciosa*) with an *alpina* clematis.

The more free-flowering *alpina* varieties can be grown horizontally along the ground. A single plant can cover an area of 3sq.m (10sq.ft) so this offers an inexpensive way of brightening up large areas. They are not, however, weed-suppressing ground cover and it will be necessary to hand-weed among the horizontal stems. At the other extreme, a free-flowering *alpina* can be grown in a container although I don't find them ideal for this purpose because their relatively short flowering period means that the extra work involved in growing them this way is scarcely worthwhile.

■ **CARE** As *C. alpina* is a native of mountains or other cold places, it is a tough plant that needs little attention once established. It is well worth giving it a little extra care when planting, however, as it has thread-like, rather fragile, fibrous roots. Don't be tempted therefore to loosen the roots to help establishment but keep the root ball undisturbed when planting and firm in gently.

■ **PROBLEMS** Generally trouble-free. They are not prone to clematis wilt and are very hardy.

Clematis **'Blue Bird'**

Clematis alpina **'Constance'**

Recommended varieties

Clematis alpina (AGM) originates from the mountains of Europe and north Asia. It has small flowers that vary from lavender-blue to purple-blue, but not all plants sold under this name are the true species. Do check with the nursery that their stock is the true AGM form.

C. alpina varieties all have nodding flowers and attractive seedheads. Their flowers are relatively small, mostly around 5cm (2in) but varying from 4cm (1½in) to 6cm (2¼in) depending on the variety.

Blue or purple-flowered varieties: 'Betina', red-purple; 'Blue Bird', mauve-blue; 'Blue Dancer', a recent introduction, similar to 'Frances Rivis' but even larger; 'Columbine', pale blue; 'Cyanea', violet-blue; 'Floralia', pale blue; 'Frances Rivis' (AGM), pale blue, very free-flowering, probably my favourite in the group, although this may because it was the first that I grew; 'Frankie', pretty inner skirt to mid-blue flowers, free-flowering; 'Helsingborg' (AGM), deep blue, almost purple, one of the strongest colours in this group; 'Pamela Jackman', deep blue; 'Prairie River', purple-blue with white at the base of the flower.

Pink or reddish-flowered varieties: 'Brunette', red-brown, attractive in bud as well as in flower; 'Constance', almost double, dark pink, raised from a seedling of 'Ruby'; 'Foxy', pale pink; 'Jacqueline du Pré', rose-mauve on the outside with a white edge, paler pink within,

very large flowers and vigorous habit; 'Pink Flamingo', semi-double, pale pink with darker veins, often flowers again in summer; 'Rosie O'Grady', pink-mauve; 'Rosy Pagoda', pale pink; 'Ruby', pink purple, flowers again in summer, a particularly vigorous variety; 'Tage Lundell', dark rose-purple; 'Willy', pale pink darker at the base, free-flowering, some flowers in summer, vigorous.

White-flowered varieties: 'Albiflora'; 'Alpina Plena', semi-double, vigorous; 'Burford White', light green foliage; 'Columbine White'

(syn. *C. alpina* 'White Columbine') (AGM), pointed sepals, very free-flowering; ssp. *sibirica* (syn. *C. sibirica*), flower colour varies from pure white to cream-white, light green foliage; ssp. *sibirica* 'White Moth' (syn. *C. macropetala* 'White Moth'), double, later flowering than most *alpinas* with light green foliage, still my favourite white-flowered *alpina* type and with especially lovely seedheads; 'White Swan' (syn. *C. macropetala* 'White Swan'), begins flowering later than most *alpina* types.

Clematis alpina **'Rosy Pagoda'**

Clematis alpina **'White Columbine'**

Clematis macropetala types

Clematis macropetala 'Maidwell Hall'

“ I like Clematis macropetala for its beauty as a garden flower. But I like it too for its history, which stretches back into one of the early periods of botanical discovery and exploration in China. Pierre d'Incarville (after whom the lovely herbaceous perennial Incarvillea was named) was one of a number of intrepid Jesuit missionaries working in and around Beijing in the middle of the 18th century. He was probably the first western-trained botanist to visit China and, although he and his colleagues were unable to travel far, he did collect plants in the mountains to the north of Beijing. Among them was C. macropetala, although he only sent back dried specimens to the West. It was evidently a plant of some note, however, and not surprisingly, it also caught the attention of the later plant collectors William Purdom and Reginald Farrer. Purdom had been collecting in China for the Veitch nursery in 1911 and sent seed of C. macropetala to them. The new clematis flowered in England for the first time in the summer of 1912. Farrer who was exploring with Purdom in 1914 also sent back material. And so a fine plant, and the most richly coloured of early clematis, came to our gardens. There are shades of both blue and red in the flowers and this has allowed a gradually widening range of variously coloured varieties to be raised over the subsequent years. ”

Clematis macropetala

PRUNING: Group 1

SITE AND SOIL: Tolerant of all aspects so very useful for cool, shady walls where some other clematis are not suitable. A moisture-retentive, slightly alkaline soil is preferred.

HARDINESS: Very hardy, tolerates at least -20°C (-4°F) in winter.

SIZE: 3-5m (10-16ft) after three or four years. They can be grown on 1-2m (3-6ft) high fences as, once they reach the top of the fence, the stems will cascade down.

PROPAGATION: Fairly easy, from semi-ripe cuttings in late summer, layering or seed.

SPECIAL FEATURES
Easy to Grow
Spring Flowers
Attractive Seedheads
Moderately Vigorous

■ **GARDEN USES** The *macropetala* varieties are very similar to the *alpina* types, slightly more vigorous but equally easy to grow. Use them around the garden as you would an *alpina* type. They are particularly useful for providing extra interest to otherwise bare and colourless areas of the garden in spring and look especially attractive when grown over low to medium-sized shrubs up to 2.5m (8ft) high. Use them for early spring interest on pergolas or arches on which roses are trained, as they will produce flowers near the base if trained up the post. Although they are suitable for growing in containers or conservatories, it is best to make the most of their hardy nature and grow them in the shadier areas or on cold walls and fences.

Alpina and *macropetala* types of clematis complement each other perfectly; both can be relied upon to come through hard winters unscathed and put on a reliable display of spring flowers.

■ **CARE** *C. macropetala* is hardy and reliable and needs little care once established. When planting, keep the root ball undisturbed and firm into the planting hole carefully so as not to damage the fibrous roots.

■ **PROBLEMS** Generally trouble-free; unlikely to be affected by clematis wilt.

Recommended varieties
C. macropetala is a native of northern China and eastern Siberia, with 5cm (2in) blue lantern-like flowers and attractive seedheads. It varies in height from 2.5-3.5m (8-11ft). Its varieties share these basic characteristics, varying mainly in flower colour and flower size, usually from 4-6cm (1½-2¼in).
Blue-flowered varieties: 'Anders, mauve-blue; 'Harry Smith', pale blue; 'Jan Lindmark' (syn. *C. alpina* 'Jan Lindmark'), mauve-purple, generally the first of the group to flower in my and most other British gardens; 'Lagoon' (syn. 'Blue Lagoon'), deep blue; 'Maidwell Hall' (AGM), deep blue; 'Pauline', bright blue flowers with long inner sepals; 'Westleton', mid-blue.
Pink-flowered varieties: 'Ballet Skirt', pale pink; 'Markham's Pink' (AGM), strawberry pink.
White-flowered varieties: 'Snowbird', pale green foliage, slow to establish; 'White Lady'.

Clematis macropetala **'Markham's Pink'**

Clematis montana

❝ *Its fans may shout, 'There's only one* Clematis montana.' *And if they were seeking an extremely vigorous clematis with flowers more than about 5cm (2in) in diameter, they would undeniably be correct. There are more vigorous clematis (*C. vitalba *and the Oriental yellow-flowered species can be monsters) but nothing else offers this combination. These characteristics should dictate how* C. montana *is grown; but they often don't. I still see houses being swamped by a* montana *planted a few years previously against a low wall, or gardeners vainly hacking back stems as thick as their wrist in the hope of still having a plant with attractive flowers. You really must plant* C. montana *where it can be offered free rein. But I wonder if this was in the mind of Lady Amherst, who brought it into British gardens from the Himalayas in 1831. Yes, it is a plant with the unusual distinction of having been introduced by a lady; and no ordinary lady. Countess Sarah Amherst was the wife of Lord Amherst, Governor-General of India from 1823-28 and she was a notable naturalist. She collected extensively in the sub-continent and, although the magnificent Lady Amherst's pheasant and the beautiful tropical Pride of Burma tree,* Amherstia nobilis *are her 'official' memorials, I always feel that her real legacy is made up of the tens of thousands of* C. montana *that glorify European gardens every spring.* ❞

Clematis montana

PRUNING: Group I
SITE AND SOIL: Tolerant of all aspects including moderate shade but always best with the top in full sun. Part of the impact of the (admittedly rather few) scented varieties is that they will release the fragrance more in a sunny position. A moisture-retentive, slightly alka-line soil is preferred.
HARDINESS: Hardy, tolerates -15 to -20°C (5 to -4°F) in winter.
SIZE: 2-3m (6-10ft) after three years, up to 8m (25ft) eventually if left unpruned.
PROPAGATION: Easy, from semi-ripe cuttings in late summer or lay-ering; not worth raising from seed because seedling plants are of very variable quality and many will flower only sparsely.

SPECIAL FEATURES
Very Vigorous
Reliably Hardy
Late Spring Flowers
Some Are Scented

■ **GARDEN USES** *Clematis montana* varieties provide quick cover but the flowering season is rather short. They are ideal, therefore, for disguising old trees, outbuildings, garage walls or chain-link fencing rather than for growing on house walls or combining with other climbers. The host plant must, however, be able to take the strain; a tree less than 8m (25ft) tall is unlikely adequately to support a fully established *montana* variety. As flowering is spectacular but brief, an evergreen host tree such as a pine or other large conifer would provide interest at other times of the year.

For growing over smaller trees, over 5m (16ft), consider the less vigorous relatives of *C. montana* such as *C. chrysocoma* or *C. vedrariensis*.

■ **CARE** The soil around a large ever-green will be very dry and it could take the clematis two to three years to become properly established. Plant 30cm (12in) away from the tree trunk and guide the clematis to the host by using a diagonal support cane. Provide extra watering and mulch, especially in the first few years. Once the clematis has become established and reaches the lowest branches, little care is needed, simply tie in any stems that become detached after flowering if you can reach them safely.

■ **PROBLEMS** More or less trouble-free. Clematis wilt is seldom a problem on *C. montana*.

Clematis montana 'Elizabeth'

Clematis montana 'Marjorie'

Clematis montana **'Tetrarose'** with *Spiraea arguta*

Recommended varieties
C. montana is a Himalayan and Chinese species with pink or white flowers. Most of its varieties reach 6-8m (20-25ft); exceptions to this are indicated under the individual descriptions. Flowers are the open type with four petaloid sepals, usually about 5cm (2in) in diameter, although some have larger flowers.
Pink-flowered varieties:
'Boughton Star', semi-double, deep cream-pink, height only 5m (16ft); 'Continuity', pink flowers on long stalks, flowers through summer and a particularly valuable variety, only recently considered a true *montana* type; many catalogues still list it as a *C. chrysocoma* hybrid; 'Elizabeth' (AGM), large flowers, pale pink, scented, very vigorous at 8-10m (25-33ft) but still to my mind the best scented *montana* clematis; 'Fragrant Spring', pink, scented, bronze foliage, very vigorous at 10m (33ft); 'Freda' (AGM), deep pink, bronze foliage; 'Gothenburg', pink with cream anthers, silver veins on foliage, height only 5m (16ft); 'Marjorie', semi-double, cream-pink; 'Mayleen', large flowers, satin pink, scented, bronze foliage, very vigorous at 8-10m (25-30ft); 'New Dawn', bright pink, very vigorous at 10m (30ft), presumably named after the climbing rose 'The New Dawn' although this shouldn't mislead you as it doesn't have the same soft pink colour; 'Odorata', pale pink, free-flowering, scented; 'Picton's Variety', deep pink, some summer flowers, bronze foliage, less

vigorous then most at 5m (16ft); 'Pink Perfection', deep pink, scented; var. *rubens* (AGM), small flowers, pink but the colour varies depending on the form, the best are mauve pink with cream stamens, young foliage is tinged with purple; 'Tetrarose' (AGM), large, round flowers, deep pink, attractive, large foliage; 'Vera', large flowers, deep pink, scented, dark green foliage, very vigorous at 10m (30ft); 'Warwickshire Rose', mid-pink with gold stamens.

White-flowered varieties: White-flowered *montana* varieties can be disappointing as there are many poor plants on the market, raised from seed. It's especially important, therefore, to seek out a good named variety from a reputable source. 'Alexander', large flowers, cream-white, scented, takes five or more years to flower but is a vigorous grower at 8-10m (25-30ft); 'Mrs Margaret Jones', small flowers, semi-double; 'Peveril', large flowers with very prominent stamens, summer flowering but flowers can still be seen above the new foliage as they are borne on markedly long stalks, like var. *wilsonii* but no scent and less vigorous at 5m (16ft); 'Superba' (syn. 'Rubens Superba'), large flowers on vigorous plants; *C.f. grandiflora* (AGM), large flowers, some forms are scented, others are not, free-flowering but very vigorous at 10-11m (30-33ft), one of the hardiest; var. *sericea* (syn. 'Spooneri', also sometimes called *C. chrysocoma* but not to be confused with the true *C. chrysocoma*) (AGM), similar to *C.f. grandiflora* but slightly later flowering; var. *wilsonii*, free-flowering, scented, flowers in summer.

Clematis montana **var. *rubens***

Clematis montana **var. *sericea***

Other early-flowering species

PRUNING: Group 1
SITE AND SOIL: A well drained soil and a sheltered, sunny position is preferred.
HARDINESS: Moderately hardy, tolerates -10 to -15°C (14 to -4°F) in winter, hybrids derived from the species tend to be more hardy.
SIZE: 5-6m (16-20ft) eventually if left unpruned.
PROPAGATION: Semi-ripe cuttings in late summer or layering.

❝ This is a group that exemplifies the global origin and appeal of clematis, embracing plants from the Himalayas, Southern China, Japan, New Zealand and western North America. Clematis chrysocoma, *a close relative of* C. montana, *has the most fascinating history. It was discovered in Yunnan in western China by the French missionary and botanist, Père Jean Delavay in 1884 and introduced to Kew by the nurseryman Vilmorin in 1910 at whose nursery the hybrid* C. x vedrariensis *originated (see opposite).* C. barbellata *from the Himalayas belongs to the same botanical group and must also be a prospect for the hybridizers. The tantalising Japanese* C. japonica *with its half-concealed flowers, the peculiar* C. afoliata *(literally, 'no-leaved clematis') from New Zealand and* C. columbiana *from the western side of North America complete a group of plants worthy of much greater attention from European gardeners.* ❞

SPECIAL FEATURES
A Less Vigorous Alternative to *Clematis montana*
Attractive Young Foliage

■ **GARDEN USES** *C. chrysocoma* and its relatives can be used for quickly covering up some unsightly object, just like their relatives derived from *C. montana*. Because of their lesser vigour, however, there is a wider choice of suitable host plants and any evergreen such as a conifer 5-8m (6-25ft) high can be used successfully.

Clematis chrysocoma

Clematis chrysocoma

Clematis x vedrariensis 'Rosea'

■ **CARE** Choosing a sheltered site and providing enough moisture to the roots in the early years are the main requirements.

■ **PROBLEMS** Generally trouble-free; not prone to clematis wilt, and so make good replacements when large flowered hybrids have failed.

Recommended varieties

C. chrysocoma originates from Yunnan in southern China. It is sometimes called the hairy clematis as the young shoots and foliage are covered with a most attractive golden-brown down. It has pale mauve-pink flowers in spring, like the *montana* varieties, but they are cup-shaped. There are usually also a few flowers borne on the new wood in summer. The young foliage is an appealing bronze. There are pink and white forms, and the rather attractive although infrequently seen plant sold simply and tantalizingly as 'a *C. chrysocoma* hybrid' has shell pink flowers with yellow stamens and bronze foliage.

C. x vedrariensis is a hybrid between *C. montana rubens* and *C. chrysocoma* raised at the famous Vilmorin nursery in Paris just before the First World War. It is similar to *C. chrysocoma* in flower and foliage shape and in its downiness but with a deeper mauve-pink flower. It is a plant of which I am particularly fond. It reaches 6m (20ft) but is less hardy than its parents. Look out especially for its varieties: 'Highdown', deep pink; 'Rosea' (syn. *C. spooneri* 'Rosea'), large, pale pink flowers.

Other species

Clematis afoliata originates from New Zealand where it is most common on South Island. It has small, tubular flowers that are cream to pale yellow and scented. The distinctive feature is its branching, rush-like stems, with the leaves reduced to leaf stalks. The habit is rather untidy, so it is best allowed to scramble between shrubs in a warm, sheltered position where it can reach 2m (6ft) in height and spread. It isn't really hardy in cold areas, although it was most famously grown by Miss Ellen Willmott in a sunny spot in her garden in Essex. It will certainly thrive in mild, seaside gardens but elsewhere should be considered barely hardy or tender.

C. barbellata originates from the western Himalayas and so, not surprisingly, is very hardy, tolerating at least -20°C (-4°F). Its flowers are like those of an *alpina* in shape but are dull purple. Height 4m (13ft). *C. b.* 'Pruinina' (syn. 'Pruinina') has lantern-shaped, plum-coloured flowers with white stamens.

C. columbiana is a western American equivalent to *C. alpina*, occurring naturally over a region south from British Columbia to Oregon and Colorado. It has nodding bells of blue to violet blue. Hardy but tricky to grow and prone to die back without obvious reason. Height 2m (6ft).

C. japonica (syn. *C. fusca*) is a Japanese species with urn-shaped flowers of purple-red to brown-red in late spring. The flowers are attractive when examined closely but they lack impact as they are often obscured by the foliage. Very hardy, tolerating at least -20°C (-4°F). Height 2m (6ft).

Clematis afoliata

❝ *I always think of these as among the most versatile of all types of clematis, for they offer a range of colours from white through mauves, pinks, reds and blues, with some bicolours and many double-flowered varieties. The main flowering period is in early summer but many repeat almost into early autumn. The flowers are usually large, often 15cm (6in) across. Yet all of these numerous and exceedingly popular summer flowering climbers are derived from one or more of only three Oriental species: Clematis florida, C. patens and C. lanuginosa, although sometimes by complex and circuitous hybridization routes.* **❞**

Clematis florida types

❝Clematis florida *is the most historic of the three species involved in the production of the early-summer-flowering hybrids. It is a native of China but had been cultivated in Japan for centuries when it was discovered growing there by the Swedish botanist Thunberg. It was introduced to European gardens in 1776. Many years later, the plant collectors Augustine Henry and subsequently Ernest Wilson found it growing in Hupeh in central China but it is obviously a rare plant in the wild. Although it's become customary to describe the varieties that I recommend below as* florida *varieties, many have their ancestry in old Japanese garden forms like 'Sieboldii' or 'Fortunei' which, it is assumed, are themselves derived from the true C. florida. A fascinating subject, but not one to worry about; enjoy these plants for their beauty, from wherever it is derived.* **❞**

PRUNING: Group 2
SITE AND SOIL: Tolerant of most aspects but almost invariably best when the bulk of the plant is in warm sun. Some light shade will produce a more intense flower colour. A moisture-retentive soil, slightly alkaline is preferred.
HARDINESS: Hardy, tolerates -15 to -20°C (5 to -4°F) in winter.
SIZE: 2-3m (6-10ft) after three or four years.
PROPAGATION: Layering is usually the easiest method. Semi-ripe cuttings in late summer are difficult to take. Seed, even if set, will yield useless seedlings.

SPECIAL FEATURES
Large Flowers
A Wide Range of Colours
A Range of Flowering Times
Moderately Vigorous

■ **GARDEN USES** The *florida* types flower mainly in late spring and early summer. If they do repeat flower later on, the flowers are usually single and, quite commonly, if these are the first flowers that gardeners see on a new purchase, they gain the impression they have been sold the wrong variety.

There is plenty of scope for using them in appropriate parts of the garden. Grow them up any small to medium-sized, free-standing or wall shrubs. Or use them very effectively to clothe a pergola or arch. The free-flowering forms are worth trying in containers and, if kept in a conservatory, they will flower even earlier.

Clematis **'Proteus'**

■ **CARE** Before planting, gently tease out any bootlace-like roots that are curling round themselves; if you can do this without disturbing the main root ball, the plant will establish more easily.

■ **PROBLEMS** Double flowers are more vulnerable to strong winds and heavy rain than singles. Careful siting, using host plants such as wall-trained shrubs for protection, or growing under cover are all ways of overcoming this problem. Clematis wilt affects all of these varieties.

ABOVE: *Clematis* 'Duchess of Edinburgh'   **BELOW:** *Clematis florida* 'Sieboldii'

Clematis 'Vyvyan Pennell'

Clematis 'Louise Rowe'

Recommended varieties

The true species *C. florida* is a deciduous or semi-evergreen plant, probably not in cultivation at present but its progeny are widely available. All have manageable vigour and double or semi-double flowers. They flower in late spring and early summer and, although there is little repeat flowering, where this does occur the blooms are likely to be single. Most flowers are 10-13cm (4-5in) in diameter; those that I have referred to as large will reach 15cm (6in).

Blue to purple-flowered varieties: 'Beauty of Worcester', double and single, deep blue with cream-yellow anthers, attractive seedheads; 'Chalcedony', double (even the later flowers), green buds open to pale silver-blue, best in semi-shade; 'Jim Hollis', double and single, silvery lavender-blue; 'Kathleen Dunford', semi-double and single, rose-purple; 'Kiri Te Kanawa' double, deep blue with cream anthers, very free-flowering; 'Teshio', double, lavender-blue, spider-like buds, a very free-flowering Japanese variety; 'Vyvyan Pennell' (AGM), large flowers, double, semi-double and single, first flowers are lavender-blue, the later ones lilac, probably the strongest growing and arguably the best double clematis.

Pink to mauve-flowered varieties: 'Belle of Woking', double, silver-mauve, attractive seedheads; 'Louise Rowe', double, semi-double and single, pale mauve; 'Proteus', large flowers, double, semi-double and single, mauve-pink, free-flowering, an extremely popular variety; 'Walter Pennell', large flowers, semi-double and single, deep mauve-pink with cream anthers.

White-flowered varieties:

C. florida 'Flore Pleno' (often listed in catalogues as 'Alba Plena'), white with tints of green, double, needs a sheltered site; *C. florida* 'Sieboldii' (syn. *C. f.* 'Bicolor'), white with purple centre but it can revert to white, free-flowering but needs a sheltered site; this is a fascinating variety, an old Japanese garden plant that reached England via Siebold's Dutch nursery in 1836; 'Arctic Queen', large flowers, fully double, cream-white, free-flowering and vigorous; 'Duchess of Edinburgh', double; 'Sylvia Denny', semi-double and single.

Clematis patens types

❝ Clematis patens *must have given rise to more varieties than any other wild clematis species and our summer gardens would be immeasurably poorer without its contribution. It is very similar in appearance to* C. florida *and at various times, botanists have thought it merely a variety. Unlike* C. florida, *however, it grows wild in both Japan and China but it was first discovered for the West growing in a garden near Yokohama by the Dutchman Siebold who introduced it into Britain in 1836. Its white or bluish flowers soon caught the serious attention of plant breeders and the introduction of an old Japanese garden variety called 'Standishii', which Robert Fortune added in 1861, gave a further impetus to a flow of new selections and hybrids that was to continue unabated until the present.* **❞**

PRUNING: Group 2

SITE AND SOIL: Most are tolerant of all aspects but are best when the bulk of the plant is in warm sun. Some varieties produce a more intense flower colour when not in full sun. A moisture-retentive soil, slightly alkaline is preferred.

HARDINESS: Hardy, tolerate -15 to -20°C (5 to -4°F) in winter.

SIZE: 2-3m (6-10ft) after three or four years.

PROPAGATION: Layering is usually the easiest method. Semi-ripe cuttings in late summer are difficult to take. Seed, as with all large-flowered hybrids is generally not set and even when it is viable, gives rise to worthless plants.

SPECIAL FEATURES
Large Flowers
A Wide Range of Colours
A Range of Flowering Times
Moderately Vigorous

Clematis 'Bees' Jubilee'

Clematis 'Kakio'

■ **GARDEN USES** The *patens* group is very large and offers a very wide choice in flower colour. Their long flowering period and moderate vigour makes the varieties feasible and attractive options even for small gardens.

Free-standing and wall-trained shrubs of any size up to 4m (13ft) can act as hosts and there is no need to restrict possible hosts to evergreens as many deciduous shrubs are equally suitable. Pergolas and arches will set off the flowers well, and they can be successful with climbing roses. All types are suitable for containers or conservatories but the compact, free-flowering varieties will provide the most impact.

■ **CARE** Before planting, gently tease out any bootlace-like roots that are curling round themselves; if you can do this without disturbing the main root ball, the plant will establish more easily.

■ **PROBLEMS** Generally trouble-free but, like all the large-flowered hybrids they can be vulnerable to clematis wilt. Mildew can also be a problem on the later flowers.

TOP: *Clematis* 'Lasurstern'
BOTTOM: *Clematis* 'Doctor Ruppel'
OPPOSITE: *Clematis* 'Miss Bateman'

Clematis **'Moonlight'**

Clematis **'Lincoln Star'**

Clematis **'Lord Nevill'**

Recommended varieties

C. patens occurs naturally with blue and white flowers. Its varieties tend to flower in late spring and early summer then, like those of the *florida* group, not usually again until the early autumn. If the flowers reach 15cm (6in) or more in diameter, I have described them as large.

Blue-flowered varieties: 'Alice Fisk', pale blue with dark brown stamens; 'Annabel', mid-blue with a white centre; 'Blue Diamond', sky blue with white stamens; 'Countess of Lovelace', double and single, pale lavender-blue; 'Daniel Deronda' (AGM), single and semi-double, violet-blue, a very reliable and popular variety; 'Edouard Desfossé', pale blue, attractive seedheads, compact and free-flowering; 'Etoile de Malicorne', large flowers, blue with mauve bar, free-flowering; 'Etoile de Paris', large flowers, mauve blue, attractive seedheads, compact; 'Gabrille', lilac blue; 'Joan Picton', lilac with lighter bar, attractive seedheads, compact and free-flowering; 'Lady Londesborough', pale blue, attractive seedheads, compact and free-flowering; 'Lasurstern' (AGM), large flowers, deep lavender blue with wavy edges, attractive seedheads, arguably the best in the group; 'Lord Nevill' (AGM), large flowers, deep blue with wavy edges, attractive seedheads; 'Minister', lavender-blue with purple stamens, compact; 'Mrs P. B. Truax', periwinkle blue, attractive seedheads, compact and free-flowering; 'Multi Blue', double, outer sepals deep blue, inner ones, blue to red, a rather

Clematis **'Multi Blue'**

extraordinary sport from 'The President' but not stable and liable to revert; 'Souvenir de J. L. Delbard', bright blue with purple stripe; 'Ulrique', blue with rose-mauve tinge and red anthers.

Mauve or purple-flowered varieties: 'Anna Louise', large flowers, violet with a red bar, free-flowering yet compact; 'Herbert Johnson', large flowers, red mauve, compact and free-flowering; 'Kathleen Wheeler', very large flowers, mauve purple with golden anthers, attractive seedheads but prone to wind damage in exposed sites; 'Marcel Moser' large flowers, mauve with deeper bar, attractive seedheads; 'Mrs N. Thompson', deep purple-blue with scarlet bar, compact and free-flowering; 'Myj', violet-purple with dark bar and creamy anthers; 'Percy Picton', large flowers, mauve with rosy flush and brown-red anthers; 'Richard Pennell' (AGM), very large flowers, blue-purple with yellow anthers, attractive seedheads; 'Royal Velvet, rich velvet purple with dark red anthers, compact and free-flowering; 'Sir Garnet Wolseley', large flowers, mauve-blue, attractive seedheads and compact; 'Sugar Candy', very large flowers, pink-mauve with darker bar and yellow anthers; 'Tateshina', violet-blue with rose-mauve bar and yellow stamens, compact and free-flowering; 'The President' (AGM), large flowers, deep purple-blue, unusual for the group in having a very long flowering season, almost continuous throughout the summer, a strong grower and overall an

Clematis **'Daniel Deronda'**

outstanding and justifiably very popular clematis; 'The Vagabond', deep purple with reddish bar and cream-yellow stamens, compact; 'Violet Elizabeth', double, mauve-pink with yellow stamens.

Pink or red-flowered varieties: 'Anna', large flowers, rose-pink, compact and free-flowering; 'Asao', large flowers, deep pink with darker edges, attractive seedheads, compact and free-flowering; 'Barbara Dibley', large flowers, red with carmine bars, attractive seedheads; 'Barbara Jackman', mauve-red with red bar and yellow anthers, attractive seedheads; 'Bees Jubilee' (AGM), large flowers, mauve-pink with deeper bar, attractive seedheads, free-flowering; 'Charissima', very large flowers, cerise-pink with a deeper bar, attractive seedheads; 'Doctor Ruppel' (AGM), large flowers, deep rose-pink with darker bar, free-flowering, one of the very best of the varieties to have appeared over the past 25 years; 'Empress of India', very large flowers, rosy cream-red; 'Gladys Picard', large flowers, mauve-pink with a deeper pink bar and golden stamens; 'Helen Cropper', large flowers, pale pink with deeper pink markings giving a raspberry ripple effect; 'Kakio' (syn. 'Pink Champagne'), large flowers, purple-pink, attractive seedheads, compact and free-flowering; 'Keith Richardson', deep crimson with a white centre; 'Lincoln Star', large flowers, raspberry pink with deeper bar but the later flowers are paler, attractive seedheads; 'Lucie' (although strictly it should be 'Lucey' as it isn't named after a girl but was found in the garden of a Mr Lucey), pink-lilac with brown stamens; 'Miss Crawshay' semi-double and single, rose-mauve; 'Peveril Pearl', pale lavender with a pink flush, needs partial shade for the best flowers; 'Scartho Gem', large flowers, bright pink with deeper bar, compact and free-flowering; 'Souvenir du Capitaine Thuilleaux' (syn. 'Capitaine Thuilleaux'), large flowers, cream-pink with deeper bar, attractive seedheads, compact and free-flowering; 'Sugar Candy', large flowers, pink-mauve with darker bar and yellow anthers with pink-grey filaments, free-flowering; 'Trianon', bright red.

White-flowered varieties: 'Gillian Blades' (AGM), wavy edges; 'Ishobel', large flowers, white with pale yellow centres and maroon stamens; 'Lemon Chiffon', cream, almost yellow with yellow anthers, compact habit, attractive foliage, the flowers are better in some shade; 'Margaret Wood', large flowers, ivory white tinged with blue and a dark centre; 'Miss Bateman' (AGM), attractive seedheads, compact and free-flowering; 'Moonlight' (syn. 'Yellow Queen'), large flowers, cream, almost yellow, attractive seedheads; 'Mrs George Jackman' (AGM), semi-double and single, attractive seedheads; 'Snow Queen', large flowers, red stamens, the later flowers often have a pale pink stripe, compact and free-flowering; 'Wada's Primrose', very similar to 'Moonlight'.

ABOVE: *Clematis* 'The President'　　　　**BELOW:** *Clematis* 'Snow Queen'

Clematis **'Lady Caroline Nevill'**

Clematis lanuginosa types

❝ Clematis lanuginosa, *the third of the Oriental trio of species, is the most mysterious of the three although probably, overall, the most important in the development of the large-flowered hybrids. It's a blue-flowered Chinese species, first found by Robert Fortune in 1850 but, in its original form, it may no longer exist, either in the wild or in cultivation. Its spirit certainly lives on, however, in many beautiful varieties. Although closely related to* C. florida *and* C. patens, C. lanuginosa *is a much shorter plant, barely 2m (6ft) tall and this restrained size is one of the features that it has contributed to the cultivated forms. It also seems responsible for the desirable characteristic of flowering in late spring or early summer and then, on and off, through the summer. Less desirably, it has also been held responsible for the susceptibility to clematis wilt of many large-flowered varieties.* ❞

Clematis **'Général Sikorski'**

PRUNING: Group 2

SITE AND SOIL: Tolerant of most aspects but best when the bulk of the plant is in warm sun. Some shade will produce a more intense flower colour in some varieties. A moisture-retentive soil, which is slightly alkaline is preferred.

HARDINESS: Hardy, tolerates -15 to -20°C (5 to -4°F) in winter.

SIZE: 2-3m (6-10ft) after three or four years.

PROPAGATION: Layering is usually the easiest method. Semi-ripe cuttings in late summer are difficult to take. Seed, even if viable, is likely to result in worthless plants.

SPECIAL FEATURES

Large Flowers
A Wide Range of Colours
A Range of Flowering Times
Moderately Vigorous

■ **GARDEN USES** To show off the large flowers, these hybrids are best grown up a pergola or an arch. Because of their formal appearance, however, they are also very successful when grown on a house wall, on a trellis or with a wall-trained shrub. Most sizes of free-standing shrubs can act as hosts. The large flowers will also be especially appreciated if they are grown in a container and if the container is kept in a well lit conservatory, flowering will be earlier. The varieties described as free-flowering and compact are those that I consider to be the best for containers.

Clematis 'Lawsoniana'

■ **CARE** Before planting, gently tease out the bootlace-like roots if they are growing around the root ball. This will help the plant establish more easily.

■ **PROBLEMS** Clematis wilt is the major problem. All the varieties known to be most susceptible have *C. lanuginosa* in their parentage.

Clematis **'Marie Boisselot'**

Recommended varieties

C. lanuginosa seems to have been an old blue-flowered Chinese garden plant. It is the parent of many large-flowered varieties that bloom in late spring and early summer and then on and off again through the summer. All are single flowered unless I have stated otherwise and have stamens of white, gold, brown or purple that contrast most attractively with the overall flower colour.

All the flowers are big in this group, reaching 10-13cm (4-5in) across but those that are 15cm (6in) in diameter I have described as large, those that attain 15-18cm (6-7in), very large.

Blue-flowered varieties: 'Beauty of Richmond', very large flowers, pale lavender-blue; 'Belle Nantaise', very large flowers, lavender-blue; 'Blue Gem', very large flowers, pale lavender-blue with dark stamens; 'Four Star', very large flowers, pale lavender with a deeper bar; 'Fuji-musume', powder blue with yellow anthers, compact and free-flowering; 'Général Sikorski' (AGM), large flowers, deep blue, free-flowering, particularly vigorous; 'Glynderek', double and single, deep blue; 'Haku-ôkan', large flowers, violet-blue with white anthers, attractive seedheads; 'Hybrida Sieboldii' (syn. 'Ramona'), large flowers, pale blue with red centre, attractive foliage, needs a sunny spot to flower well; 'Ken Donson', (AGM), large flowers, deep blue with yellow anthers; 'Lady Caroline Nevill', large flowers, semi-double and single, pale lavender-blue, particularly vigorous; 'Lady Northcliffe', Wedgwood blue, compact and free-flowering; 'Lawsoniana', very large flowers, lavender-blue; 'Mrs Bush', very large flowers, lavender-blue; 'Mrs Cholmondeley' (AGM), very large flowers, light lavender-blue, a mass of flowers over a long season, attractive seed-heads; 'Mrs Hope', large flowers, pale blue with dark red anthers; 'Sealand Gem', lavender with dark pink bar; 'Violet Charm', very large flowers, pale violet-blue with red anthers; 'W. E. Gladstone', very large flowers, blue with dark red anthers; 'Will Goodwin' (AGM), very large flowers, pale blue deeply veined and with wavy edges; 'William Kennet', large flowers, lavender-blue; 'Yvette Houry', large flowers, double and single, pale blue, free-flowering.

Mauve or purple-flowered varieties: 'Edomurasaki', large flowers, deep purple-blue with red anthers; 'Guiding Star', very large flowers, light purple with dark stamens; 'Kacper', very large flowers, intense violet with dark stamens; 'King Edward VII', large flowers, mauve with pink bar; 'Lilacina Floribunda', deep purple; 'Maureen', rich deep purple; 'Princess of Wales' (an old variety named after Queen Alexandra and not to be confused with the *texensis* variety 'Princess Diana' (syn. 'The Princess of Wales') (see page 79)), very large mauve flowers, vigorous and free-flowering; 'Silver Moon' (AGM), large

Clematis **'Mrs Cholmondeley'**

Clematis **'Otto Froebel'**

Clematis **'Princess of Wales'**

flowers, silver-mauve, compact and free-flowering; 'Susan Allsop', dull magenta with red bar and yellow stamens; 'Veronica's Choice', large flowers, double and single, pale lavender and mauve, compact; 'Wilhemina Tull', large flowers, deep purple with red stripe.

Pink or red-flowered varieties: 'Carnaby', deep pink with darker bar, attractive seedheads, free-flowering; 'Crimson King', very large flowers, crimson with brown anthers; 'Fairy Queen', very large flowers, light pink with rose bar; 'John Warren', very large flowers, deep pink with darker edges, not for a windy position; 'King George V', large flowers, sometimes semi-double, pink with dark bar; 'Ruby Glow', very large flowers, ruby rose-mauve with red anthers, compact and free-flowering; 'Sympathia', very large flowers, rose-lilac with brown stamens.

White-flowered varieties: 'Edith' (AGM), compact; 'Henryi' (AGM), very large flowers, free-flowering; 'Marie Boisselot' (syn. 'Madame le Coultre') (AGM), very large flowers, probably the most famous and possibly the best white-flowered clematis ever raised; 'Otto Froebel', very large flowers with wavy sepals and brown stamens.

Clematis **'Ruby Glow'**

Clematis **'Silver Moon'**

Clematis **'William Kennett'**

Related early flowering types

I've included here a range of good, and some extremely good, varieties that have mixed parentage. All have either Clematis lanuginosa *or* C. patens *in their ancestry somewhere; some have both but others, including* C. viticella *and* C. 'Jackmanii' *have contributed too. The group includes the variety 'Nelly Moser' which, although not the best, is probably the best known of all clematis.*

Clematis **'Elsa Späth'**

PRUNING: Group 2

SITE AND SOIL: Tolerant of most aspects but best when the bulk of the plant is in warm sun. Flower colour is often more intense in light shade. A moisture-retentive soil, slightly alkaline is preferred.

HARDINESS: Hardy, tolerates -15 to -20°C (5 to -4°F) in winter.

SIZE: 2-3m (6-10ft) after three or four years.

PROPAGATION: Layering is generally the easiest form of propagation. Semi-ripe cuttings in late summer are difficult to take and seed, even if viable will result in worthless plants.

Clematis **'Pagoda'**

SPECIAL FEATURES

Large Flowers
A Wide Range of Colours
A Range of Flowering Times
Moderately Vigorous

■ **GARDEN USES** These varieties are used and cared for in the same way as the *patens* and *lanuginosa* types.

■ **PROBLEMS** Susceptibility to clematis wilt is the biggest problem, and this is passed on through the C. *lanuginosa* parent.

ABOVE: *Clematis* **'Nelly Moser'**   **RIGHT:** *Clematis* **'Royalty'**

Recommended varieties
Blue or purple-flowered varieties: 'Bracebridge Star', large flowers, lavender-blue with carmine bar, attractive seedheads; 'Elsa Späth (syns. 'Blue Boy', 'Xerxes') (AGM), very large flowers, mid-blue, a mass of flowers over a long period, a quite excellent older variety; 'Fireworks' (AGM), blue-mauve, deep red bar, free-flowering; 'H F Young' (AGM), Wedgwood blue, attractive seedheads, compact and free-flowering; 'Mrs James Mason', double then single, violet-blue with red bar and cream stamens; 'Prins Hendrik', very large flowers, blue with red anthers; 'Royalty' (AGM), semi-double and single, rich purple-mauve with yellow anthers, compact; 'Star of India' (AGM), deep purple-blue with carmine bar, very free-flowering.

Pink or mauve-flowered varieties: 'Boskoop Beauty', deep rose with red-purple bar, a notable Dutch variety; 'Corona' very large flowers, light purple-pink with dark red stamens; 'Horn of Plenty' (AGM), very large flowers, rose-mauve with a deep bar, compact and free-flowering; 'Nelly Moser', large flowers, pale mauve with deep lilac bar, compact and free-flowering, perhaps the most famous of all clematis with its huge flowers and very striking barred appearance; 'Pagoda', small nodding flowers, pink-mauve, has *viticella* in its parentage, the explanation for the smaller flowers.

White-flowered varieties: 'Dawn', white with pink, attractive seedheads, compact and free-flowering; 'Fair Rosamond', white with pink bar, scented, attractive seedheads, compact and free-flowering; 'Guernsey Cream', cream or almost yellow, compact and free-flowering; 'James Mason', clear white with dark red anthers; 'Titania', very large, white with purple-pink stripe and brown stamens.

LATER SUMMER-FLOWERING HYBRIDS

Jackmanii types

66 *The name 'Jackmanii' must be one of the most familiar in the clematis world. Even gardeners who know little about the genus will have heard of it. Rather fewer, however, know the history of this plant, its special merits or how it acquired its unusual name. Jackman's of Woking in Surrey was one of the great plant nurseries of the 19th century. Among their breeding plants was* Clematis lanuginosa *(in the days, of course, when it still existed) and in one series of crosses, it was pollinated by* C. viticella *'Atrorubens' and also by* C. x eriostemon *'Hendersonii'. Seed was collected and the resultant plants flowered for the first time in 1862. Two distinct forms were selected and made commercially available; the better form was called* C. x jackmanii, *the plant we know today simply as 'Jackmanii'. It is almost certain that the* C. viticella *pollen fathered this superb hybrid. By coincidence, a similar cross was made around the same time in France. The great significance of these crosses was that the combination of the European* C. viticella *with the Asiatic* C. lanuginosa *resulted in plants with rich, lush flower colours and a long flowering period. Today, the Jackmanii group includes a great many, sometimes rather complex hybrids involving other Asiatic species but they are usefully grouped together since they all share a European-Asiatic ancestry and a long flowering season.* 99

PRUNING: Group 3

SITE AND SOIL: Tolerant of most aspects but best when the bulk of the plant is in warm sun, although the flower colour is usually more intense if the head is in light shade. A moisture-retentive, slightly alkaline soil is preferred.

HARDINESS: Hardy, tolerates -15 to -20°C (5 to -4°F) in winter.

SIZE: 2-3m (6-10ft) after three or four years.

PROPAGATION: Layering is generally the easiest method. Semi-ripe cuttings in late summer are difficult to take. Seed, even when viable, will give rise to worthless plants.

Clematis **'Ascotiensis'**

Clematis **'Comtesse de Bouchaud'**

Clematis 'Ernest Markham'

LATER SUMMER-FLOWERING HYBRIDS

Stunning Colours
Long Flowering Period
Moderately Vigorous

■ **GARDEN USES** These clematis produce their flowers on the current season's growth. They can be planted to grow over a wide range of host plants and objects but look best when allowed to scramble informally over walls, fences, tree stumps, pergolas, arches and similar structures.

Roses traditionally make stunning partners to Jackmanii clematis. The most popular of all clematis at the present time, the variety 'Perle d'Azur', grown with a pink climbing rose is a classic combination. Any size of host plant is suitable, from low spreading shrubs to trees. The rich purple and red-flowered varieties will brighten up grey-leaved shrubs of all sizes.

The Jackmanii varieties are the ideal climbers to accompany and grow through spring-flowering shrubs, as they will have been pruned back hard and so be out of the way while the host is in flower and will then grow up to take over the flowering interest in summer. The same principle can be applied to winter-flowering heathers: if a Jackmanii variety is allowed to wander over the heathers, it will liven them up in summer. Then, by pruning back the clematis hard in winter, you will give the heathers centre stage when they come into flower.

The habit of these varieties isn't suitable for growing in containers as the flower are produced towards the ends of rather long shoots, though their long-flowering period might tempt you to train them.

ABOVE: *Clematis* 'Hagley Hybrid'   **RIGHT:** *Clematis* 'Jackmanii'

Clematis **'Jackmanii Superba'**

■ **CARE** It is very important to remember to prune these clematis hard in late winter or early spring or they soon become an unruly tangle. Pruning too soon, in early winter, can encourage growth if the weather is mild. This new growth will then be vulnerable to later cold spells, which can damage the buds or the flowers. The most frustrating problem with the Jackmanii clematis is that all of the flowers are at the top while the base of the plant is bare. A Jackmanii variety will never flower near the base, as the young wood must grow and mature before it can bear the flowers.

■ **PROBLEMS** Jackmanii types are susceptible to clematis wilt but not to the same extent as the *lanuginosa* group. In common with other later-flowering clematis, mildew can be a problem in some years. Red-flowered varieties seem more prone to mildew and can also fade badly in the sun. Choose your site carefully and spray with a suitable preventative fungicide.

Clematis 'John Huxtable'

Clematis 'Niobe'

Recommended varieties

The original 'Jackmanii' itself is still sold, still widely available and is one of the most easily recognisable varieties. There are also many excellent new forms derived from or related to it. Most of the flowers are 10-13cm (4-5in) in diameter but I have indicated any that have larger flowers.

Blue or purple-flowered varieties: 'Ascotiensis' (AGM), bright blue, free-flowering; 'Christian Steven', light blue; 'Esperanto', purple with contrasting bar; 'Gipsy Queen' (AGM), velvet violet-purple with dark red anthers; 'Jackmanii Superba', slightly larger flowers than 'Jackmanii', velvet purple; 'Jackmanii (AGM), dark velvet purple, the original variety; 'Jubileinyi 70', velvet violet with light brown centre; 'Luther Burbank', violet-purple with paler bar and yellow stamens; 'Madame Grang' (AGM), velvet purple; 'Marie Louise Jensen', violet-blue, long sepals; 'Miriam Markham', large flowers, semi-double, lavender; 'Nikolai Rubtsov', red-violet with yellow stamens, free-flowering; 'Perle d'Azur' (AGM), sky blue, free-flowering, the biggest selling clematis of the present day and possibly of all time; 'Phjanael' (syn. 'North Star'), mid-blue with deeper bar; 'Prince Charles', mauve-blue, compact and free-flowering; 'Rhapsody', sapphire blue with cream-yellow anthers, deeper blue as sepals age, free-flowering; 'Romantika', very large flowers, dark violet with yellow stamens; 'Serenata', large flowers, dusky purple with yellow anthers, free-flowering; 'Sputnik', various shades of blue; 'Victoria', rose-purple; 'Viola', blue-violet with greenish yellow stamens, free-flowering; 'Warszawska Nike', rich purple with yellow stamens.

Pink or mauve-flowered varieties: 'Caroline', soft rose, deeper pink at the base, free-flowering; 'Colette Deville', mauve-pink with red and cream centre; 'Comtesse de Bouchaud' (AGM), mauve-pink, free-flowering; 'Dorothy Walton', mauve-pink, free-flowering; 'Hagley Hybrid', mauve-pink, a late pink variety, compact and free-flowering; 'Jackmanii Alba', semi-double and single, pale mauve to grey; 'Jan Pawel II' (syn. 'John Paul II), pale white-pink with red anthers; 'Madame Baron Veillard', rose-lilac, very late so needs a particularly sunny spot to ensure flowering; 'Margaret Hunt', dusky mauve-pink, free-flowering and vigorous; 'Pink Fantasy', pale pink with brown anthers, darker bar.

Red-flowered varieties: 'Allanah', bright red with black-red anthers;

Clematis **'Perle d'Azur'**

'Jackmanii Rubra', semi-double and single, red-purple; 'Kardynal Wyszynski' (syn. 'Cardinal Wyszynski'), crimson with dark anthers; 'Madame Edouard André' (AGM), dusky red; 'Monte Cassino', vivid red with cream stamens; 'Niobe' (AGM), large flowers, dark red, masses of flower over a long period; 'Rouge Cardinal', velvet crimson, free-flowering; 'Rüütel', very large flowers, dark pink-red with red stamens; 'Sunset', red with purple, yellow anthers, very long flowering; 'Twilight', petunia mauve, free-flowering yet compact; 'Vino', very large flowers, red with cream-yellow anthers.

White-flowered varieties: 'Bella', white with cream bar, red anthers, free-flowering, for the best flower colour choose a semi-shady spot; 'John Huxtable', free-flowering; 'The Bride', white with cream centre, long flowering, flowers are better in semi-shade; 'Tuczka', white with bright yellow stamens.

Related hybrids

'Blekitney Aniol' (syn. 'Blue Angel'),
sky blue with darker, crimped edges,
very free-flowering; 'Ernest Markham'
(AGM), magenta, it needs full sun for
a good flower display, one of the few
reds not to fade in the sun; 'Lady Betty
Balfour', large flowers, violet-blue,
flowers very late so plant in a sunny
spot to ensure a good display.

RIGHT: *Clematis* **'Prince Charles'**
BELOW: *Clematis* **'Rouge Cardinal'**
OPPOSITE: *Clematis* **'Warszawska
Nike'**

CLEMATIS VITICELLA AND RELATIVES

Clematis viticella

❝ *If I could grow only one type of clematis, I am fairly certain that I would choose a* viticella *variety. It's hard to define what I find so special about them: their blooms aren't large, they don't have particularly unusual colours and they aren't the longest-flowering varieties. What they do offer is a simplicity that I find appealing, their colours are especially rich and deep and they are almost the only medium-sized, open-flowered types to continue the clematis theme until well into the autumn. Clematis viticella is a European plant. It occurs naturally in the south, from Italy eastwards; and not surprisingly, therefore, it is among the species that have been longest in cultivation. The existence of a double-flowered variant was recognised at an early date and the London herbalist John Gerard, writing in 1597 in his 'Grete Herball' said of both single and double forms that 'they grow in my garden in Holborn and flourish exceedingly'. They flourish exceedingly in my garden too and a very large number of varieties have now joined the basic types. Along with my favourite of all 'Madame Julia Correvon', the rich purple variety 'Royal Velours' has been an outstanding* viticella *for many years, joined recently by 'Polish Spirit' a rather similar plant that very swiftly and justifiably collected an AGM.* ❞

PRUNING: Group 3
SITE AND SOIL: Tolerant of all aspects, so they are particularly useful for cool, shady walls and fences. A moisture-retentive, slightly alkaline soil is preferred.
HARDINESS: Hardy, tolerates -15 to -20°C (5 to -4°F) in winter.
SIZE: 3-4m (10-13ft) after three or four years.
PROPAGATION: Relatively easy from semi-ripe cuttings in late summer or by layering.

SPECIAL FEATURES

Some Lovely Reds
Long Flowering
Ideal Partners for Roses
Moderately Vigorous

■ **GARDEN USES** These clematis are particularly easy to grow and their long flowering period makes them invaluable additions to the garden. They are suitable for many types of support; those with nodding flowers are especially effective when grown into the branches of small trees where you can look up at them. Their long flowering period and tolerance mean they can be used to brighten up fences and walls of any aspect. As they are pruned hard in winter, they can be used like the Jackmanii types to add summer interest to spring-flowering shrubs, and are especially effective when allowed to ramble through heathers.

The white-flowered varieties are particularly attractive when grown in the same way as that lovely herbaceous climber, *Tropaeolum speciosum*: over a dark evergreen hedge such as yew. The red and purple-flowered varieties would combine will with yellow-variegated evergreen shrubs. These clematis also make excellent partners to climbing roses on pergolas or arches.

■ **CARE** The *viticella* varieties are easy to care for as long as you remember to prune them hard in winter.

■ **PROBLEMS** Generally trouble-free. Virtually free from clematis wilt but the later flowers can suffer from mildew in dry summers.

Clematis viticella **'Purpurea Plena Elegans'**

Clematis **'Alba Luxurians'**

Recommended varieties

C. viticella is a southern European species that has contributed much to the range of varieties available today. It has been used as a parent for both large and small-flowered varieties but the true species is also still well worth growing. The varieties are only moderately vigorous and so are readily kept under control. Most have simple, single flowers up to about 5-6cm (2-2¼in) in diameter; I have indicated in the individual descriptions those that are larger or have a nodding habit. *C. viticella* itself is a valuable garden plant but you should be sure to see it in bloom before buying, as the quality of the flowers varies greatly. Select a form with a rich, deep purple flower and avoid those that are a dull grey-purple. Flower shape should be distinct; either nodding or open but not half-way between the two.

Blue or purple-flowered varieties: 'Betty Corning', pale blue, scented, nodding flowers; 'Blue Belle', very large flowers, deep violet-blue, slightly nodding; 'Elvan', purple with cream stripe, nodding with slightly twisted sepals; 'Etoile Violette' (AGM), large flowers, violet-purple with yellow anthers, free-flowering; 'Mrs T. Lundell', blue-lilac, nodding

Clematis 'Etoile Violette'

Clematis 'Madame Julia Correvon'

Clematis **'Margot Koster'**

flowers with slightly recurving sepals; 'Polish Spirit' (AGM), large flowers, rich purple-blue, free-flowering; 'Royal Velours' (AGM), deep velvet purple; *C. viticella* 'Mary Rose', double, blue-mauve; *C. v.* 'Purpurea Plena Elegans' (AGM), double, violet-purple, nodding flowers.

Pink or red-flowered varieties: 'Abundance', wine rose with deeper red veins and cream-green stamens, nodding flowers, free-flowering; 'Carmencita', clean light red; 'Kermesina', dark red; 'Madame Julia Correvon' (AGM), large flowers, bright rose-red with cream-yellow stamens, slightly nodding, I still think this is the best *viticella* type and I'm not at all sure that it isn't my favourite of all clematis; 'Margot Koster', large but gappy flowers, rose-pink, slightly nodding, looks better from a distance; 'Sôdertälje' (syn. 'Grandiflora Sanguinea'), very large flowers, deep pink, slightly nodding and gappy.

White-flowered varieties: 'Alba Luxurians' (AGM), large flowers, white with green tips and dark purple stamens, nodding; 'Little Nell', cream-white with pink flush, slightly nodding; 'Minuet' (AGM), white with mauve markings, slightly nodding; 'Tango', white with red markings; 'Venosa Violacea' (AGM), large flowers, white with purple markings.

C. viticella relations with large flowers

The following varieties have a *viticella* parent but their flowers are generally larger, often earlier and the pruning advice for them varies. These varieties tend to be listed in catalogues under the heading 'large-flowered hybrids' and are best used in the garden in the same way as the true large-flowered hybrids. They grow to a height of 2.5-3m (8-10ft) unless I have stated otherwise. I have described them as large when the flowers are 15cm (6in) in diameter and given individual pruning advice.

Blue or purple-flowered varieties: 'Emilia Plater', bright blue with cream stamens, summer to early autumn flowering, pruning Group 3; 'Maskarad' (syn. 'Masquerade'), very large flowers, mauve-blue with mauve bar and dark red anthers, early summer and then late summer to early autumn flowering, pruning Group 2; 'Perrin's Pride', large flowers, purple with green bronze centre, overlapping sepals, early summer to early autumn flowering, height 3.5m (12ft), although a Group 3 type requiring hard pruning, the flowers are larger on the old wood so you can prune half of the plant hard and then prune the remainder lightly; 'Saturn', large flowers, lavender-blue with maroon bar and white stamens, early summer and early autumn flowering, pruning Group 1.

Pink or red-flowered varieties: 'Duchess of Sutherland', large flowers, dark red with cream stamens, summer flowering, pruning Group 2; 'Mrs Spencer Castle', large flowers, semi-double and single, pink, summer flowering, pruning Group 2; 'Ville de Lyon', bright crimson with yellow anthers, summer to early autumn flowering, height 3m (10ft) if hard pruned (pruning Group 3) or 9m (30ft) if lightly pruned (pruning Group 2); 'Voluceau', petunia red with yellow anthers, twisted sepals, summer flowering, pruning Group 3.

White-flowered varieties: 'Huldine', smaller flowers than others in this section (only 7.5cm (3in) in diameter), white with pale mauve bars on the reverse of the sepals, summer to early autumn flowering, very vigorous with a height of 5-6m (16-20ft), pruning Group 3.

C. viticella relations with a herbaceous habit

These are late-flowering clematis with a flower similar to the *viticella* types, but they have the habit of their herbaceous parent *Clematis integrifolia* (page 82), and are best treated in the same way. They are sometimes described as non-clinging but it is possible to encourage them to 'drape' over a host plant such as a medium-sized shrub. All flower from summer to early autumn and are in pruning Group 3.

C. x durandii (AGM) is a cross between *C.* 'Jackmanii' (through which it derives its *viticella* connection) and *C. integrifolia*, made around 1870 in Lyons, flowers 7.5cm (3in), deep indigo blue, height 1.5m (5ft); *C. x eriostemon* (syn. *C. hendersonii*) is a cross between *C. integrifolia* and *C. viticella*. The typical form is sometimes seen; it was raised in France and given this name around 1852. It has purple-blue, slightly

nodding flowers, height 2.5m (8ft) but varieties derived from other crosses are better and more widely available. *C. x eriostemon* 'Blue Boy', pale blue, is one but *C. x eriostemon* 'Hendersonii' (syns. *C. hendersonii*, *C. integrifolia* 'Hendersonii'), is the most beautiful of all and a quite outstanding plant, dark purple blue, and raised in England, before the typical French form, in around 1830.

LEFT: *Clematis* 'Ville de Lyon'   ABOVE: *Clematis x durandii*   *Clematis x eriostemon* 'Hendersonii'

LATE-FLOWERING SPECIES

After midsummer, a group of rather distinct clematis, very different from the large-flowered hybrids, come into their own. Their flowers are much smaller, but have their own charm, being dainty and often bell- or lantern-shaped. The vigour varies depending on the species from which they are derived. They fall into the following four groups although the first three are frequently confused and the names are used differently in different catalogues: there are three Orientals, *Clematis tangutica*, *C. tibetana* and *C. orientalis* and one North American, *C. texensis*.

Clematis tangutica **'Lambton Park'**

Clematis tangutica

" There are six or seven fairly widely cultivated plants with the specific name 'tangutica'. An Allium, *a* Daphne, *and this* Clematis *are the best known. The name derives from the Tanguts, an ethnic Tibetan people who live in the borderland of north-eastern Tibet and the Kansu region of China.* C. tangutica *occurs over a fairly wide area of Central Asia and was originally described by a man who, for a considerable period in the middle of the 19th century, after the time of Robert Fortune, was the great authority on Chinese plants. He was Carl Maximowicz, of the Botanic Gardens in St Petersburg. He was clearly an intrepid explorer and it's been said of him that 'he collected far off the beaten track among the hills in a manner that Fortune ... never dared to do'. It wasn't until 1898, however, after Maximowicz's death, that this fine yellow clematis was introduced from St Petersburg to Kew. The form that we usually see today derives from a later collection from western Kansu, made by the English collector William Purdom in 1911. Now that these Oriental species are so familiar to us, it's hard to imagine the impact they must have made when first seen. They are remarkably different from those clematis types grown hitherto and although for some gardeners, there is a great deal of foliage for such small flowers, I continue to find the overall impact extremely impressive. "*

Clematis 'Helios'

■ GARDEN USES These clematis are very straightforward to grow in most gardens and their yellow flowers and attractive seedheads add interest to the garden in autumn and winter. They are best used where they can grow unrestricted so use them to cover large walls, pergolas, arches or, best of all, fairly large trees (up to about 8m/25ft) although they are likely to swamp anything smaller. One notable exception is the compact new variety 'Helios', which attains little more than to 1-2m (3-6ft) and so can be grown over shrubs and fences.

■ CARE The plants are tough but, as they have fibrous roots, plant them carefully without disturbing the root-system. The main task is the annual hard pruning.

■ PROBLEMS Generally trouble-free. They are much less likely to suffer from clematis wilt than the large-flowered hybrids.

PRUNING: Group 3
SITE AND SOIL: Tolerant of all aspects. Best with some sun but can tolerate shade better than other species in this group. A moisture-retentive, slightly alkaline soil is preferred.
HARDINESS: Hardy, tolerates -15 to -20°C (5 to -4°F) in winter.
SIZE: Established plants reach 3-4m (10-13ft) each year, even with hard pruning. Unpruned, they can easily attain 5-6m (16-20ft).
PROPAGATION: Can be easily propagated, either from semi-ripe cuttings in late summer, by layering or, in some instances, from seed. I have raised a number of batches of plants from purchased seed, however, and have to say that I have been pretty disappointed with the results. The plants are variable (not in itself a bad thing) but I have yet to find one that is as good as an existing named form.

SPECIAL FEATURES
Nodding, Bell-Shaped Flowers
Very Easy to Grow
Vigorous

Clematis tangutica

Recommended varieties

Clematis tangutica itself is still the most commonly-grown and the most recognisable form with its small, 3cm (1in) nodding yellow flowers from late summer to autumn. Most plants on sale are raised from seed so the shade of yellow will vary and it's important to buy your plant in flower in order to see exactly what you are purchasing. *C. tangutica* can reach 5-6m (16-20ft) in height even if pruned hard.

The following varieties have larger flowers than the species. All are at least 4cm (1½in) in diameter, while those 5cm (2in) or over I have described as large. There are also slight differences in flowering time. All have attractive seedheads. 'Gravetye Variety', small flowers, yellow, free-flowering; 'Lambton Park', large flowers, bright yellow; var. *obtusiuscula*, small flowers, yellow; 'Aureolin' (syn. *C. tangutica* 'Aureolin') (AGM), large flowers, yellow, free-flowering, height 4-5m (13-16ft); 'Bill MacKenzie' (syns. *C. orientalis* 'Bill MacKenzie', *C. tangutica* 'Bill MacKenzie') (AGM), yellow, free-flowering, vigorous, attaining 6m (20ft), one of the best as the flower display can last into early winter; 'Burford Variety, yellow, thick sepals, vigorous, attaining 6m (20ft), flowering can continue into early winter; 'Corry', large flowers, lemon yellow; 'Golden Tiara', bright golden yellow, compact at 2.5m (8ft); 'Helios', large flowers, bright yellow, very compact at 1-2m (3-6ft).

ABOVE: *Clematis* 'Bill MacKenzie'

RIGHT: *Clematis tibetana*

Similar species

Clematis tibetana, as its name suggests, originates from Tibet and also from Nepal. Its flowers are not particularly exciting, being a greenish yellow-orange colour, and plenty of sun is needed for them to open in quantity. The foliage is fern-like and an attractive blue-green and the rather striking seedheads are really the most outstanding feature. Height 5m (16ft).

C. tibetana ssp. *vernayi* (syn. *C. orientalis*) (AGM) is popularly known as the orange peel clematis due to its remarkably thick, fleshy sepals of green yellow to burnt orange. Height 4.5m (15ft). There are three variants:

C. tibetana ssp. *vernayi* 'Orange Peel' (syn. *C. orientalis* 'Orange Peel'), *C. tibetana* ssp. *vernayi* LS & E 13342 (syn. *C. orientalis* 'Sherriffii') and *C. tibetana* ssp. *vernayi* var. *laciniifolia*. To add to the confusion that exists in catalogues over the naming of this group, I have seen all variants sold simply as 'Orange Peel Clematis'. The name LS & E 13342 is the collection number given to the plant by its collectors (Ludlow, Sherriff and Elliott) who first introduced the plant from the Himalayas in 1947. It is an unusual instance of a plant collected in the wild that proved to be a good garden plant yet was never properly named and continues to be identified simply by its number.

Clematis tibetana ssp. vernayi

Clematis chiisanensis

YELLOW-FLOWERED SPECIES

C. aethusifolia, from northern China and Korea, has lovely lace-like, ferny foliage and is only 2m (6ft) high. The pale yellow flowers are small but are produced from summer until early autumn.

C. akebioides, from western China, is rather like *C. orientalis,* being vigorous at 5m (16ft) with masses of small, greenish yellow flowers. Sometimes the flowers are stained red or purple beneath.

C. chiisanensis, from Korea, is similar to *C. tangutica* but is not easy to grow. If you succeed, the reward will be a dramatic display of large, silvery seed-heads. Height 4m (13ft).

C. connata does not start to flower until late summer or autumn when there is a brief display lasting only a few weeks. The flowers are showy, cream-yellow bells 3-4cm (1-1½in) long. A vigorous plant from the Himalayas

Clematis rehderiana

and south western China, growing to 5m (16ft).

C. intricata (syn. *C. glauca*) is similar to *C. akebioides* but with attractive foliage more like *C. orientalis*. It comes originally from northern China and southern Mongolia.

C. ladakhiana, originally from Kashmir, has unusual flowers, the colour of old gold and speckled with dark red, the stamens are maroon and the anthers dull yellow. It flowers late and needs plenty of sun to ensure a good display. Height 4.5m (15ft).

C. orientalis (syn. *C. ispahanica*) was the first of the group to be introduced to western gardens, and arrived as long ago as 1731 although it is, in its true form, a relatively unattractive species with dingy green-yellow flowers on vigorous plants up to 8m (25ft). Be aware that other, better plants are sometimes sold under this name. It has a widespread origin from the Aegean and Ukraine to Iran, the Himalayas, western China and Korea.

C. rehderiana (syn. *C. buchananiana*) (AGM) originates from western China and has small yellow bell-shaped flowers. Its special attribute is its sweet scent, sometimes said to resemble that of cowslips and it is certainly, in my experience, the most pleasantly fragrant of the group. Very vigorous, reaching 6-8m (20-25ft) so best for larger gardens.

C. serratifolia is an attractive species with masses of star-like flowers and lush green foliage. The flowers are a clear primrose yellow with purple stamens but unfortunately they are retained for only a short time in the autumn. Height 3m (10ft). It originates from Korea and north-eastern China.

WHITE-FLOWERED SPECIES

C. apiifolia, from China and Japan, has groups of small, rather dull white flowers in autumn. Height up to 4.5m (15ft). Moderately hardy.

C. chinensis is a good autumn-flowering species from central and western China. It has scented flowers 3-4cm (1-1½in) across and flowers well if given a sunny spot. Height 5m (16ft).

C. gracilifolia from western China, has 5cm (2in) flowers in summer, and it reaches a height of 4m (13ft).

C. grata is a very vigorous climber from the Himalayas reaching 10m (30ft). It has masses of small, cream-white flowers in autumn.

C. potaninii (syn. *C. fargesii*) has a distinctive satin-like texture to its flowers. A Chinese species, it is vigorous, reaching a height of 5m (16ft) but never seems to flower prolifically in cultivation. Moderately hardy. *C. potaninii* var. *potaninii* (syn. *C. potaninii* var. *souliei*) is a larger-flowered form.

Clematis potaninii **var. souliei**

Other Oriental types

These species may be difficult to obtain even from clematis specialists but they do include some fascinating plants. All are hardy unless otherwise stated and are in Pruning Group 3.

Clematis fusca is an oddity from north-eastern Asia. It has small, deep chocolate brown flowers covered in short hairs, and attractive seedheads. It reaches around 2.5m (8ft) and forms a woody framework unless pruned hard each year. *C. fusca* ssp. *fusca* (syn. *C. fusca* var. *kamtschatica*) is similar. *C. fusca* var. *violacea* (syn. *C. ianthina*) from Korea is a purple-flowered variant.

C. mandschurica (syn. *C. terniflora* var. *mandshurica*) from China and Japan, only reaches 1.2-1.5m (4-5ft). It tends to be non-clinging initially but, rather like many ivies, forms a mound of growth and then begins to grow up a support. It produces masses of small, white, star-shaped flowers from summer to early autumn. If planted in a sunny place it produces an aniseed scent.

C. terniflora (syns. *C. maximowicziana*, *C. paniculata*, *C. thunbergii*), is another scented, white-flowered species from Japan. This one is more vigorous, growing to 6m (20ft) so hard pruning is needed. It will flower best if placed in a sunny spot.

European species

PRUNING: Group 3
SITE AND SOIL: Tolerant of any aspect but best when the bulk of the plant is in sun and the roots shaded. A moisture-retentive slightly alkaline soil, is preferred.
HARDINESS: Hardy, tolerate -15 to -20°C (5 to -4°F) in winter.
SIZE : Most reach 4-5m (13-16ft) even if hard pruned; some are even more vigorous.
PROPAGATION: Semi-ripe cuttings in early to midsummer or, in most cases, seed.

SPECIAL FEATURES
Autumn Flowers
Small Flowers
Some Scented

■ **GARDEN USES** These species are valuable in informal areas of the garden to provide interest late in the season. Their vigour makes them suitable for

Clematis flammula

Clematis fusca var. violacea

covering large walls, pergolas or arches. Shrubs of all sizes and trees up to 8m (25ft) make suitable hosts for the less-vigorous types; dark-leaved evergreens are particularly suitable as they show up the white-flowered varieties rather well.

■ **CARE** *C. flammula* has fibrous roots and needs to be planted carefully without disturbing the root ball. When planting them to grow over hosts, plant about 30cm (12in) away where

the soil will be less dry, and guide the clematis to the host. Provide extra water for the first couple of years. Subsequently, the main care is to remember to prune them each year.

■ **PROBLEMS** Although eventually vigorous, some take a few years to become properly established. They are not as susceptible to clematis wilt as the large-flowered hybrids.

Clematis campaniflora

Clematis x *triternata* 'Rubromarginata'

Recommended varieties

C. campaniflora is an absolutely delightful Portuguese species, closely related to *C. viticella*. A vigorous grower, it will reach 8m (25ft). The flowers are very pretty little bells of the palest lilac-blue but are very prolific from summer to early autumn. In my own garden, it grows through a large shrub rose and into a *Magnolia grandiflora*. *C. campaniflora* 'Lisboa' is similar but with slightly bigger flowers of blue-mauve.

C. flammula is known as the fragrant clematis for its rich hawthorn-like scent. It is a southern European and Middle Eastern relative of the familiar British native *C. vitalba*. Its

flowers are like a mass of milky white stars from summer to early autumn; attractive seedheads follow. It forms a fairly vigorous scrambler up to 4.5m (15ft).

C. vitalba (syn. *C. virginiana*) is the familiar 'old man's beard' of British hedgerows. Its popular name of Traveller's Joy was the invention of the herbalist Gerard who rather picturesquely said: 'Because of its decking and adorning waies and hedges where people travel, thereupon I have named it Traveller's joy'. It is not a clematis for the average garden as it can reach 9-18m (30-60ft) and the flowers are individually uninspiring. However, the silky silver

seedheads brighten up the winter landscape.

'Paul Farges' (syn. 'Summer Snow', *C.* x *fargesioides*) is a cross between *C. vitalba* and *C. fargesii*. It has prolific, small, white flowers from summer to early autumn and attractive seedheads. A vigorous variety for quick cover reaching 6m (20ft).

C. x *triternata* 'Rubromarginata' (syn. *C. flammula* 'Rubra Marginata') (AGM) is a cross between *C. flammula* and *C. viticella*. It has the form and scent of the first and the dusky pink colouring of the latter, making it a very good variety for larger gardens. Height 4.5m (15ft).

Clematis texensis

" European gardeners sometimes forget how relatively late in botanical history many of the native plants of the United States were discovered. Throughout much of the 19th century, when China was first being opened up to European plant hunters, a great deal of North America was also unexplored and wagon trains were still beating an uncertain path westwards to the Pacific. The most important of the North American clematis in gardens today is the most westerly in distribution: Clematis texensis was not discovered in its native Texas until 1850, and introduced to Britain some 18 years later. The more easterly species, however, had not surprisingly preceded it and the earliest of them to reach Europe, C. crispa arrived in 1726, its rather striking and unusual appearance clearly having caught the eye. Today, I feel that far too little attention is given to these plants by British gardeners. Certainly, they are not as hardy as the mainstay garden clematis of Chinese origin, but they are a charming and distinctive group that should be more widely appreciated. "

PRUNING: Group 3
SITE AND SOIL: Tolerant of all aspects but best given some shelter and sun. A moisture-retentive, slightly alkaline soil is preferred, but these plants are more tolerant of drier situations than many clematis.
HARDINESS: Moderately hardy, tolerates -10 to -15°C (14 to 5°F) in winter.
SIZE: 1-2m (3-6ft) after one year. When established, it will reach 2-3m (6-10ft) each year.
PROPAGATION: Fairly easy either from semi-ripe cuttings in late summer, layering or from seed.

SPECIAL FEATURES
Red-Pink Bell or Tulip-Shaped Flowers
Moderately Vigorous
Moderately Hardy

■ **GARDEN USES** The main value of these plants lies in their flower shape and colour. Their growth habit is rather sparse so they are best grown over a host plant. Choose one to create interesting flowering combinations or to extend the period of interest. Most fairly vigorous free-standing or wall shrubs are suitable. *C. texensis* is also a good plant for pergolas, pillars and arches.

■ **CARE** The species has a reputation, not entirely justified, for being somewhat tender, but it does make sense to apply a compost mulch around the crown in late autumn. They should be hard pruned each year.

Clematis **'Gravetye Beauty'**

■ PROBLEMS

Like many other late-flowering species, they can suffer from mildew, especially in dry years. They are not susceptible to clematis wilt.

Clematis **'Duchess of Albany'**

Clematis **'Etoile Rose'**

Recommended varieties

C. texensis is sometimes called the scarlet clematis or leather flower, an apt name for two special features: the blood red colour and the leathery texture of the sepals. Although the flowers are small, their form is an interesting pitcher-shape, rather like a *kaufmanniana* tulip. It flowers from summer to early autumn and its blue-green foliage is a good foil for the flowers. Height is a modest 3m (10ft) and, in Britain, the plant dies back to soil level each winter.

Its varieties are more usually seen than the species but although they offer many of the features of the species, most are shades of deep pink rather than red and not all have the blue-green foliage.

'Duchess of Albany' (AGM), the most famous and most popular form, is clear pink with rose-pink bars, upright flowers, blue green foliage; 'Etoile Rose', deep pink with nodding flowers (derived from *C. viticella*, its other parent); 'Gravetye Beauty', cherry red, upright flowers; 'Ladybird Johnson', dusky red edged with purple as the flower ages, cream-yellow stamens, blue-green foliage; 'Sir Trevor Lawrence', blue-crimson, upright flowers; 'Princess Diana' (syn. 'The Princess of Wales'), deep pink with cream-yellow stamens.

C. versicolor is closely related to *C. texensis*. It has similarly shaped flowers but they are smaller and more prolific. The buds are a strong purple-pink and as the flower opens the colour fades to mauve-pink. This species needs the protection of a warm wall in colder areas. Height 2m (6ft).

Clematis ligusticifolia

Clematis crispa

Clematis viorna

Other North American late-flowering species

Clematis crispa (syn. *C. simsii*) from the south-eastern United States is slender and only 2m (6ft) high so is suitable for growing over a small shrub. The nodding bells can vary from light blue to bluish purple, the centre is white and forms a distinct star. The edges of the flower curl up and, for this reason, it is sometimes called the curl flower or blue jasmine. Flowering is sparse but continues from summer to early autumn. Worth trying in a small, warm sheltered corner, the stems die down in winter and a thick protective mulch

will be needed. *C. crispa* 'Cylindrica' (syn. *C. crispa* 'Rosea') is similar apart from the flower colour which is rose-pink on the outside, deep pink-red within.

C. ligusticifolia (syn. *C. virginiana*) from eastern North America is an New World version of the European *C. vitalba*, less vigorous at 6m (20ft) but still only suitable for large and fairly wild gardens.

C. pitcheri (syn. *C. simsii*) originates in the southern United States. It is more tender than *C. texensis* and produces

few flowers but they are most attractive, pitcher-shaped, bluish purple on the outside and deep purple within. Attractive seedheads follow. In good conditions it can reach 3m (10ft).

C. viorna (vase vine) is a curious species from the eastern United States. The pitcher-shaped flowers vary in colour from orange-brown to red-purple with cream tips. It has attractive seedheads but is more tender than *C. texensis* and, in Britain, dies back to soil level in winter. Height 2-3m (6-10ft).

HERBACEOUS CLEMATIS

" *The notion that clematis may be anything other than climbers is still something of an alien one to many modern gardeners, although our forebears used even the fairly rampant species horizontally rather than vertically by pegging down the stems. The group that I'm concerned with here, however, are simply too short to climb and their above ground growth tends to die back in winter; they really must be grown in the same way as herbaceous perennials for that is essentially what they are. These herbaceous species are certainly in the minority (only a handful of the 230 or so in the genus) but my garden is enriched by them and they provide a fascinating contrast to anything else that you are likely to have in your borders. The most important species are* Clematis integrifolia *from southern Europe, western and central Asia,* C. heracleifolia *from central and northern China, and the longest cultivated, the southern European* C. recta, *certainly in gardens by the time that Gerard wrote of it in 1597. A number of other Oriental, European and American species have been introduced over the years too and they at last seem to be gaining some of the recognition that they deserve.* "

PRUNING: Group 3
SITE AND SOIL: A sunny spot with a moist, rich loam will produce the best results but other soils are suitable if improved to retain moisture.
HARDINESS: Hardy, tolerates -15 to -20°C (5 to -4°F) in winter.
SIZE: 75-90cm (30-34in) but some are more vigorous.
PROPAGATION: Basal cuttings in spring, simple division and layering. Seed can be collected from *integrifolia* types but the seedlings can be variable.

Clematis integrifolia

SPECIAL FEATURES
Non-Climbing Habit
Masses of Small Flowers
Many Scented

■ **GARDEN USES** Although
the herbaceous clematis produce
scrambling stems that do not climb,
they can be trained, to a limited
degree, through shrubs. Alternatively,
they are very effective when supported
with twiggy sticks or L-shaped wire
or similar stakes. Support of young
plants is tricky but becomes easier
once they are well established. In
large borders, they can simply be
allowed to sprawl between other
plants. They may be used much as
other late-flowering herbaceous
perennials are used in herbaceous or
mixed borders, to add late summer
colour and autumn seedheads. The
flowers are rather effective at attract-
ing butterflies and can also be used
for cutting; a vase of clematis flowers
in the house will always arouse

Clematis recta

Clematis 'Wyevale'

comment, even if the flowers are
short-lived.

■ **CARE** Treat as you would a normal
herbaceous plant and put supports in
place by late spring. In late autumn or,
better, in the following spring, cut back
stems to 15cm (6in) above the ground.

■ **PROBLEMS** The *heracleifolia* and
jouiniana types layer themselves when
the stems flop to the ground; this is
not necessarily a problem but the
young roots can be damaged by hoeing.
When the plants are allowed to grow
along the ground, they are very prone
to slug damage.

HERBACEOUS CLEMATIS

Recommended varieties

C. heracleifolia does not die back completely in winter but tends to leave a woody stock. The leaves are large and there are clusters of hyacinth-like flowers that vary from light to purple-blue. The named varieties usually have better flowers than the true species. All have attractive seedheads. Height is 75-90cm (30-34in) unless I have stated otherwise, although if not trained upwards they can spread to 1-1.2m (3-4ft).

'Campanile', mid-blue, height 1.2m (4ft); 'Côte d'Azur', hyacinth blue, scented; var. *davidiana*, clear lavender-blue, heavily scented, free-flowering, does not grow from a woody base; var. *davidiana* 'Wyevale' (AGM), mid-blue, scented, free-flowering and, in my experience, much the best of the group although I do find it slow to establish; 'Jaggards', deep blue.

C. integrifolia has nodding bells of purple-blue and cream-white stamens. Plants can sometimes support themselves and grow to 75cm (30in) but often the stems fall against other plants in the border or sprawl along the ground, then grow up again to 30cm (12in). Choose a named variety for the greatest flowering impact. If the flowers are 5cm (2in) or more in length, I have described them as large. 'Alba', large flowers, white scented; var. *albiflora* (syn. *C. integrifolia*) white; 'Olgae', large flowers, pale blue, scented, free-flowering; 'Pangbourne Pink', deep red-pink, free-flowering; 'Pastel Blue', large flowers, pale blue, scented; 'Pastel Pink', light pink, scented; 'Rosea' (AGM); large flowers, pink, slightly twisted sepals, scented; 'Tapestry', large flowers, mauve-red.

Clematis heracleifolia 'Cote d'Azur'

Clematis x aromatica

Newer herbaceous varieties

A number of these varieties have begun to appear in recent years; I have little personal experience of them but (predictably) the nurseries selling them commend them highly: 'Aljonushka', rose pink, with fleshy, twisted sepals, height 1.5-2m (5-6ft); 'Arabella', purple-blue with cream anthers, height 1.5-2m (5-6ft); 'Petit Faucon', deep blue with orange or yellow centre, compact and free-flowering, the young foliage is bronze-green, height 1m (3ft).

Other species

C. addisonii is one of the smallest herbaceous clematis at 30-50cm (12-20in) high and originates from the north-eastern United States. The flowers are a nodding pitcher shape, purple-red on

the outside and with cream margins to the recurved sepals. The leaves are heart-shaped and blue-green.

C. x aromatica is an old French cross between *C. integrifolia* and *C. flammula*. The flowers are a dark violet-purple with cream anthers and a strong scent, the foliage is sparse and, although this plant can reach 1.5m (5ft), without some support, it flops on to nearby plants, spreading to 1m (3ft).

'Edward Prichard' is an Australian cross between *C. recta* and *C. heracleifolia* var.*davidiana*. It bears masses of small, cream-white sweetly scented flowers edged with pink. It must have a

Clematis recta **'Purpurea'**

rich soil and sunny position to succeed. Height 1m (3ft).

C. x jouiniana (syn. *C. grata*) is a cross between *C. vitalba* and *C. heracleifolia* var. *davidiana*. It is hardy and vigorous, reaching 2-3m (6-10ft) and forming a woody framework. There is an abundance of small flowers, which are off-white but deepen to lilac or sky blue towards the tips. Two varieties particularly worth seeking out are: 'Mrs Robert Brydon', off-white flowers tinted with blue, and 'Praecox' (AGM), pale blue, flowers earlier and for longer, can be used as ground cover.

C. koreana is a Korean species with dull violet or red-brown flowers like small nodding bells. The leaves are rather large and coarse. Height 2.5m (8ft). f. *lutea* is a pale yellow variant; var. *fragrans* has shiny red-brown flowers and a cedarwood scent.

C. recta is a popular central and southern European species with various forms, differing greatly in their height and flowering impact. Height is 1-2m (3-6ft) but all plants need support or they will flop. The flowers resemble small white stars, but vary in quantity between strains and some are scented, others are not. The seedheads are attractive. It is worth looking for the following named varieties: 'Grandiflora', large flowers, white, free-flowering; 'Peveril', large flowers, white, scented, free-flowering, a dwarf form at 1m (3ft) high; 'Purpurea', small white flowers, purple foliage; ssp. *recta* var. *lasiosepala* (syn. *C. hexapetala*), small flowers, white, bell-shaped, foliage reminiscent of mistletoe. Height 30-60 cm (12-24in).

C. songarica originates from a wide area covering Mongolia, Korea, south Siberia and Turkestan. It forms a woody-based perennial up to 1.5m (5ft) high. There are masses of tiny white flowers, each like a star with red anthers, and the foliage is an attractive grey-green.

C. songarica var. *songarica* is a striking Siberian species bearing pure white flowers with yellow stamens, followed by attractive seedheads. It has bamboo-like stems that reach to a height of 1-1.2m (3-4ft). Plant in a sunny spot to enhance the almond scent.

C. stans originates from Japan and is a close relative of *C. heracleifolia*. The small, pale blue flowers are borne in clusters and followed by attractive seedheads. Like most scented clematis, it must be planted in a sunny spot to bring out the fragrance. The foliage is rather large and coarse. Height 60-90cm (24-36in).

Clematis x jouiniana

Clematis x *jouiniana* '**Mrs Robert Brydon**'

Clematis x *jouiniana* '**Praecox**'

Clematis koreana f. *lutea*

EVERGREEN CLEMATIS AND TENDER SPECIES

66 *Were it not for one, by now well known and much admired species, it would never occur to most European gardeners that clematis were anything other than deciduous. We have to thank two of the greatest of plant collectors for the exception to this general belief. The French naturalist, Père Armand David was collecting in western Sichuan in China in around 1873 when he found a vigorous, evergreen, white-flowered and fragrant clematis with rich green, rather leathery leaves. He sent seeds to the Paris Museum where his compatriot Adrien Franchet named it in his honour. Then in 1889, the Englishman Ernest Wilson set off on his first collecting expedition to China. He concentrated his collecting around Ichang on the Yangtze river in western Hupeh and garnered an astonishing harvest of wonderful species. The dove tree,* Davidia involucrata, Stranvaesia (= Photinia) davidiana, *(both also honouring David),* Cotoneaster dammeri, Acer griseum; *the list goes on, and it too includes the glorious evergreen* Clematis armandii. *Wilson's plants were then made available for cultivation through Veitch's nursery. I can certainly imagine the excitement the plant hunters must have felt on finding this plant in the wild in China, as I have seen it festooning the huge and fantastic rocks of the so-called 'stone forest' at Lunan in Yunnan.*

Most evergreen clematis, except C. armandii, *are too tender to be grown successfully outdoors in other than milder areas or sheltered positions, but they can, of course, be grown as conservatory or greenhouse plants. And if they are grown in containers, they can be used in the summer garden and then brought under cover before the first frosts. The New Zealand and other southern-hemisphere species are best treated as plants for the alpine house although some of the more hardy types could be considered for a rock garden* 99

Clematis armandii

Clematis armandii

PRUNING: Group 1
SITE AND SOIL: Needs a sheltered, warm, sunny wall. A moisture-retentive, slightly alkaline soil is preferred.
HARDINESS: Fairly hardy, tolerates -5 to -10°C (23 to 14°F) in winter.
SIZE: 1-2m (3-6ft) after one year, 4-5m (13-16ft) ultimately.
PROPAGATION: The easiest method is to layer the plants as, like many evergreens, they are difficult to raise from cuttings. Seed-raised plants are very variable.

Recommended varieties

C. armandii is the hardiest evergreen species and has dark green glossy foliage. In spring, there is a mass of large, white, beautifully scented flowers. It is a strong, vigorous grower, reaching at least 4-5m (13-16ft) even with pruning. The young foliage is often beautifully bronze-coloured but it is worth seeking out one of the named forms; although their habit is similar, the flowers are even better: 'Apple Blossom', pink buds opening to white flowers, scented; var. *biondiana,* cream, scented, slightly narrower foliage; 'Bowl of Beauty', white, bowl-shaped flowers, scented; 'Jeffries', white, scented, long pointed leaves, sometimes flowers again in summer; 'Snowdrift', large flowers, pure white, highly scented.

SPECIAL FEATURES
Scented Flowers
Good for a Sheltered Spot
Some Year-Round Appeal

■ **GARDEN USES** *C. armandii* grows best when not confined, so if possible you should allow it to ramble informally. The ideal spot is if you have a sunny, sheltered wall. Otherwise, try it up a pergola or large pillar. It can be grown in a large conservatory border where you would be able to appreciate the perfume, although the flowers are untidy when they drop.

Clematis armandii **'Apple Blossom'**

Other Chinese species

C. napaulensis (syns. *C. foetida,* *C. forrestii*) is found in northern India and south-western China. An interesting feature of this plant is that it is wintergreen rather than evergreen so, rather perversely, it loses its leaves in summer and new growth starts again in the autumn. The leaves don't have the usual leathery texture but are more delicate in appearance. Clusters of bell-shaped, yellow flowers with purple anthers are produced in winter. It is easily kept to 3m (10ft) if grown in a container and pruned after flowering.

C. uncinata can be considered a less vigorous, but also less hardy, alternative to *C. armandii* as it only reaches 3-4.5m (10-15ft). The flowers are less striking, being only half the size and they appear later in the summer but are scented. The foliage is attractive and blue-green.

C. fasciculiflora bears clusters of yellow-white flowers and grows to 6m (20ft).

Clematis cirrhosa

PRUNING: Group I
SITE AND SOIL: Needs a sheltered, warm, sunny wall. A moisture-retentive, slightly alkaline soil is preferred.
HARDINESS: Barely hardy, tolerates 0 to -5°C (32 to 23°F) in winter.
SIZE: 1-2m (3-6ft) after one year, 4-5m (13-16ft) ultimately but only in favourable areas.
PROPAGATION The easiest method is to layer the plants as they are difficult to raise from cuttings.

SPECIAL FEATURES

Unusual Freckled Flowers
Good for a Sheltered Spot
Some Year-Round Appeal

Clematis cirrhosa

■ **GARDEN USES** Unless you have a sunny, sheltered wall, it is best grown in a container in a conservatory.
■ **PROBLEMS** Cold winds can damage the foliage, buds and flowers. Where it grows well, it will fill out at the top and leave the lower stem rather bare.

Clematis cirrhosa var. balearica

Clematis forsteri

Recommended varieties

C. cirrhosa (syn. *C. calycina*) originates from southern Europe and the Mediterranean. In the wild, it is a vigorous scrambler but in gardens it generally grows little more than around 4.5m (15ft). The winter flowers make this is a highly desirable plant although usually there are also summer flowers on young wood. The flowers are bell-shaped, about 4cm (1½in) in diameter, cream with red-brown spotting. There are a number of named varieties, which tend to flower a little later: var. *balearica* (AGM), has foliage that turns bronze in winter and is more finely divided than that of the species, hence the common name fern-leaved clematis; var. *balearica* is similar but with even more finely divided foliage; 'Freckles' (AGM) is a striking plant with larger flowers, cream pink with red-purple spots; 'Jingle Bells', cream buds, pure white flowers, vigorous to 4.5-6m (15-20ft); 'Wisley Cream', similar to the species but with no spotting on the flowers.

Clematis cirrhosa 'Freckles'

New Zealand and other Southern Hemisphere species

All the New Zealand clematis are dioecious, that is male and female flowers are found on different plants. They have been used to produce some very showy hybrids.

C. forsteri (syn. *C. hexapetala*) has attractive, finely divided foliage and spring or early summer flowers. The flowers are lemon-scented but are otherwise unremarkable being small, slightly nodding and yellow or green-yellow. Height 2m (6ft).

'Green Velvet' is a cross between *C. australis* and *C. petriei* 'Princess', a female selection. Stronger growing than the parents, it is said to be hardy and reaches 1.5-2m (5-6ft). It is a striking male plant with lime-green flowers, scented and free-flowering.

'Lunar Lass', a cross between *C. marata* and *C. x marmoraria*, is a female plant with cream-green flowers and green foliage trailing to 25cm (10in); may be grown as an alpine or worth trying in a sheltered spot in well-drained soil. 'Moonman' is a male form from the same cross, larger white flowers, better but not as easy, grow it as an alpine in a pan or trough.

C. indivisa (syn. *C. paniculata*) has male flowers 5-10cm (2-4in) across, white with orange-pink anthers. The female flowers are smaller, white with sterile green filaments. Both sexes are borne on large panicles in spring and summer and the plants are then covered with flower. An ideal conservatory plant, it can be kept to 2-3m (6-10ft). 'Fairy' is a female form. *C. hookeriana* closely resembles *C. indivisa* but has green-yellow to light yellow flowers.

C. marata is a low evergreen climber with green-yellow flowers; male and female forms are available.

C. marmoraria (AGM) is a quite fascinating plant, the smallest clematis at only 6cm (2 ¼in). Its foliage looks more than anything like a stiff clump of parsley. The flowers are green-white, ageing to cream-white. Moderately hardy.

Clematis indivisa

Clematis marmoraria

Clematis x cartmanii

C. aristata is an Australian species with masses of small white flowers in spring. A vigorous grower to 6m (20ft).

C. brachiata is South African and can used as a conservatory plant. It has scented, white flowers, tinted green, and golden stamens from late summer to early autumn. It can attain 2m (6ft).

C. gentianoides is an unusual bushy clematis from Tasmania. In spring or summer, there are white, star-shaped flowers. It needs a sunny, well-drained spot in the garden and winter protection, or can be grown in a container. Height 50cm (20in).

C. hilariae (syn. *C. chrysocoma* var. *paucidentata*) a tender species from South America, is a vigorous climber with white flowers.

C. microphylla is a tender Australian climber with cream flowers. Height 5m (16ft).

C. petriei is a scree-growing scrambler with dark green foliage. The flowers are scented, cream-green bells and are followed by attractive seedheads. In Britain it grows to 60cm (24in) against a wall or fence; in its native New Zealand it can reach 4m (13ft). 'Limelight' is a male selection with lime-green flowers and purple foliage; 'Princess' is a female selection, similar to 'Limelight' but with smaller flowers and showy seedheads.

C. x cartmanii is a cross between *C. marmoraria* and *C. indivisa* resulting in a bushy dwarf, intermediate between the parents. It has finely divided foliage and large panicles of white flowers in spring. 'Joe' is a wonderful male selection worth seeking out for the sheer abundance of white flowers that cover the 30cm (12in) plant. Said to be barely hardy, to -5°C (23°F) it is usually grown in a pan in an alpine house, where it can either be trained upwards on a cane, or allowed to cascade down. However, several British nurseries report that it can be grown outside; one suggests pegging down the lateral shoots to prevent wind damage.

Clematis gentianoides

INDEX

PHOTOGRAPHIC ACKNOWLEDGMENTS

All photographs appearing in this book were specially commissioned from Andrew Lawson, except the following:

A-Z Botanical Collection /Ian Gowland 74 top; **Garden Picture Library** /Philippe Bonduel 73 top, /Howard Rice 29 left, /J.S. Sira 80 , 91 bottom; **Garden & Wildlife Matters** 81 right, /John Feltwell 51 bottom, 52 bottom left, 81 left; **John Glover** 87 top, 91 top, 92 bottom right; **Reed Consumer Books Ltd**. /Steve Wooster: F jkt inset, 32 , 88; **Photos Horticultural** 28 , 29 right, 36 left, 37 , 48 top, 70 , 87 bottom right, 93 top, 93 bottom; **Andrew Lawson Photography** 36 right, 38, 39 bottom, 41 left, 41 right, 42 top, 44 bottom left, 44 right, 45 , 49 , 55 , 73 bottom, 74 bottom, 75, 76 left, 85 left, 86, 87 bottom left, 90 left; **Harry Smith Collection** 52 bottom right, 72 Treasures of Tenbury Ltd. /Charles Chesshire 52 top.

With special thanks to the following who allowed their gardens to be photographed:

Mike Brown, Shillingford, Oxford; The Bull Inn, Charlbury, Oxford; Daphne Clark, Charlbury, Oxford; Clifton Nurseries, London; Mrs Day, Hatch Beauchamp, Somerset; Docton Mill, Devon; The Garden House, Buckland Monachorum, Devon; The Gawen House, Devon; Gothic House, Charlbury, Oxford; Hadspen Gardens, Somerset; Hatch Court, Somerset; Libby Hollinshead, Leafield, Oxford; Simon & Antonia Johnson, Middle Chinnock, Somerset; Mart Llewellyn, Shaftesbury, Dorset; John Meares, Norton-sub-Hamdon, Somerset; Angela Neville, Welcombe, Devon; Mirabel Osler, Ludlow, Shropshire; Mrs Joan Phillips, Leafield, Oxford; The Priory, Charlbury, Oxford; RHS Flower Show, Chelsea 1997; RHS Gardens, Rosemoor, Devon; Marianne & Alastair Robb,Cothay Manor, Somerset; Dr James Smart, Marwood Hill, Devon; Angela Towers, Charlbury, Oxford; Rosemary Verey, Barnsley House, Glos.